Freedom and Its Limitations in American Life

DAVID M. POTTER

Freedom and Its Limitations in American Life

Edited by Don E. Fehrenbacher

With a Bibliography of the Published Works of David M. Potter
Compiled by George Harmon Knoles

STANFORD UNIVERSITY PRESS

Stanford, California

Stanford University Press
Stanford, California
© 1976 by the Board of Trustees of the
Leland Stanford Junior University
Printed in the United States of America
Cloth ISBN 0–8047–0933–5
Paper ISBN 0–8047–1009–0
Original edition 1976
Last figure below indicates year of this printing:
87 86 85 84 83 82 81 80 79 78

Contents

Editor's Preface

IN LATE January and early February 1963 David M. Potter delivered the Commonwealth Fund Lectures in American History at University College, London. His subject, as announced in a three-page syllabus, was "The Compulsions of a Voluntaristic Society: Individual Freedom and Its Limitations in American Life." The honor of participating in this renowned lecture series was one that he could not easily have refused, and yet it came at a difficult time.

After nineteen years of teaching history at Yale, Potter had moved to Stanford in 1961 at the age of fifty, losing ground, as a consequence, in his unending struggle to catch up with his scholarly commitments. The obligation that weighed most heavily on him was a contract signed in 1954 to write the volume on the coming of the Civil War for Harper's New American Nation series. He had arrived at Stanford with the book already long overdue and still well short of completion. Habitually a man of his word, he suffered considerable embarrassment from having several times promised and failed to deliver the manuscript on a specified date. "I feel a humiliation about it which makes it hard for me to write to you now," he told one of the editors of the series in November 1961. "After what has passed, I do not see how I can give you any date you could feel any confidence in." Nevertheless, before closing the letter, he ventured to name the end of

the following April as his new "target date." The penalty
for this imprudence was having to draft another contrite
letter when spring came. "My position," he wrote, "is
quite like that of a defaulting debtor who has no assets
on which his creditors can foreclose. . . . Like all debtors,
I have had more than one creditor, and have been trying
more or less desperately to pay the smaller creditors because I thought they could be taken care of more easily."
Accordingly, he had published six "essay-length pieces"
during the preceding two years, and four more were
awaiting publication. With all of that work cleared away,
Harper now constituted his "first creditor," and if he
could maintain the same rate of production, "the end
of August would be a safe expectation." Again his unrealistic deadline rushed to meet him, and in September
1962 he sent off another "message of humiliation," re-
porting that despite good progress he was "still in the
trenches." At this point, as he prepared to begin his second year of teaching at Stanford, the Commonwealth
Fund Lectures lay just four months ahead.

The Harper book would still be unfinished when Potter died in 1971. He never put it aside for long and never
entirely stifled a Micawberish hope that the end of it
would turn up one day in a burst of creative activity. (In
1964, for example, he laid out a timetable for drafting
the final six chapters in sixty days, with an additional
thirty days to be allowed for "revision and putting in
footnotes.") This long ordeal of authorship places him
disarmingly within a circle of human frailty that includes
many another eminent scholar; one is reminded especially
of Frederick Jackson Turner's struggle to finish *his* volume in the *old* American Nation series. Yet it is also important to note that Potter's difficulties with the Harper
project grew in part out of the very qualities that won
him recognition as a historian of the first rank. His pas-
sion for excellence progressively extended the length of

the book and slowed the pace of his writing; for it required that each chapter reflect a total mastery of the often enormous secondary literature and at the same time glow with new meaning extracted from familiar material. Meanwhile he became, if anything, increasingly amenable to interruptions. The single-mindedness needed to complete the book on a set schedule was incompatible with the range and vitality of his professional interests and with his constitutional reluctance to decline any intellectual challenge.

The Harper volume covering the antebellum period had been assigned to Potter largely on the strength of his highly praised first book, *Lincoln and His Party in the Secession Crisis* (1942). But the year in which he accepted the assignment and thereby committed so much of his future to a relatively limited historical theme was coincidentally the same year, 1954, in which he published his second major book, *People of Plenty: Economic Abundance and the American Character*, a work of such impressive scope and interpretative power that it signalized virtually a second beginning of his scholarly career. The Civil War era continued to hold his undiminished interest, but always in competition with other historical themes and problems that somehow captured his attention. *People of Plenty* established Potter as an authority on the American national character and on the disciplinary connections between history and the social sciences. There naturally followed a succession of invitations to review books, deliver lectures, and participate in conferences related to those specialties. Thus he accumulated some of the "small creditors" that were triumphantly paid off in the early 1960's, only to be swiftly replaced. Potter's scholarship by then had in fact settled into an unintended but more or less permanent pattern of alternation between slow, magisterial progress on the Harper book and spirited engagement in what he sometimes called "forays," exploring subjects such as modern advertising, women in American history, and the implicit assumptions of practicing historians.

In the Commonwealth Fund Lectures, prepared after a summer of very hard work on the Harper book, Potter further pursued his interest in national character with special reference to the complex problem of freedom in American society. His point of departure was the contrast between our own picture of ourselves as the "freest people on earth" and the emphatic judgment of Tocqueville that certain kinds of freedom were severely limited in the United States. Potter found the first elements of an explanation in the tendency of Americans to associate liberty primarily with their rejection of coercive authority— a rejection both embodied and symbolized in the revolt against George III. The lectures accordingly developed into a scrutiny of the social and psychological consequences of that rejection, and more particularly, of the surrogate compulsions that evolved to do work once done by overt authority. As one might expect from the man and his subject, Potter did not end up resolving the disagreement over American freedom with which his investigation had begun; instead he incorporated it into a configuration of paradox that offered neither easy comfort nor reason for despair.

Potter apparently gave the lectures much preliminary thought and had their general structure clearly in mind, but he did not allow enough time for composition. The handwritten pages from which he read each lecture are obviously a first draft, to some extent lacking the tight organization and literary polish of his published work and lapsing occasionally into mere outline. Only after extensive revision would the manuscript have been suitable for publication, and the pressure of other commitments no doubt discouraged the effort if he ever seriously considered it. The lectures were therefore stored away in his files, though one finds parts of them echoed in later writings.

Publication is ventured now for several reasons. First of all, Potter has himself become a subject for historical study as a figure of some prominence in the intellectual history of his time, and these lectures constitute a revealing chapter in the development of his thought. Furthermore, the lectures were delivered near the end of a distinctive era from which we are now separated by the chasm of the Vietnam War, and their content in certain ways faithfully reflects the perspectives, interests, and moral concerns of critical-minded Americans in the 1950's. Yet the central theme of the lectures lends them an abiding relevance, and they are committed to print primarily because of the light of wisdom they cast on that noble idea and elusive condition called freedom.

In preparing the lectures for publication I found myself driven by two conflicting purposes that had to be reconciled. One was the determination to preserve as much of Potter's own phrasing as possible; the other was the conviction that I must edit the manuscript with as much rigor as he would have brought to bear in doing so. The result has been some measure of compression, rearrangement, and revision, amounting at times to uninvited collaboration. But the concepts, structure, and language remain substantially those of the author. Publication was undertaken with the consent and cooperation of Catherine M. Potter. My editorial task would have been much more difficult without the counsel of J. G. Bell and without assistance from the staff of the Department of History at Stanford. Everyone interested in David M. Potter and his contributions to the literature of American history will share my gratitude to George Harmon Knoles for compiling the comprehensive bibliography of Potter's published works.

Freedom and Its Limitations
in American Life

CHAPTER ONE

Freedom from Coercion

LEONARDO DA VINCI'S *Mona Lisa*, on loan from the Louvre, was unveiled recently in a private ceremony at the National Gallery in Washington. For the occasion, President John F. Kennedy had prepared a speech in which he said that this was the "second lady" sent by France to the United States, the first having been the Statue of Liberty in New York harbor. But the audience of invited guests set up such a tumult that scarcely anyone could hear the President's graceful words. A cynic might say that if Mr. Kennedy's speech illustrated the American commitment to liberty in theory, the behavior of the crowd illustrated one aspect of the American concept of liberty in practice. For Americans have traditionally been convinced that the United States is a sanctum of liberty, and Europeans have traditionally questioned whether American liberty is not, in practice, more a freedom to make noise than a freedom of the spirit.

It was long ago that inhabitants of the United States became notorious for congratulating themselves incessantly on their liberty. Mrs. Trollope wrote in 1831, for instance, of the "eternal boast of liberality and the love of freedom" that she encountered among the Americans. Harriet Martineau quoted a Bostonian assertion in 1835 that talk about liberty had become "almost a wearisome cant," and that American speeches and journals were "made nauseous by the vapid and vainglorious reiteration." Even so friendly a critic as Lord Bryce declared, "Americans cherish the notion that they are the only people who enjoy true political liberty, liberty far fuller than that of England, far more orderly than that of France."[1]

But one need not rely on the testimony of visitors from beyond the seas for evidence of the American emphasis on liberty. The Declaration of Independence asserted it as a self-evident truth that all men are entitled to liberty, along with life and the pursuit of happiness. The Constitution was ordained "to assure the blessings of liberty." The American national anthem celebrated the Republic as "the land of the free." Abraham Lincoln, in his Gettysburg Address, justified a war of subjugation on the ground of the need to preserve a Union "conceived in liberty." Franklin Roosevelt used the phrase "freedom-loving nations" to designate the members of the grand alliance against the Axis powers. One could go on and on quoting expressions which show that Americans have consistently believed themselves the "freest people on earth."

Yet as I have suggested, this central tenet of the American credo has never gone unquestioned among Europeans. Perhaps its outstanding challenger was Alexis de Tocqueville, for he first clearly set forth the idea that Americans subordinated the principle of freedom to the principle of equality. "Liberty," he said, "is not the chief and constant object of their desires; equality is their idol:

1. Frances Trollope, *Domestic Manners of the Americans* (Vintage ed.; New York, 1949), p. 221; Harriet Martineau, *Society in America* (2 vols.; New York, 1837), II, 199; James Bryce, *The American Commonwealth* (2 vols.; London, 1888), II, 635.

they make rapid and sudden efforts to obtain liberty and, if they miss their aim, resign themselves to their disappointment; but nothing can satisfy them without equality, and they would rather perish than lose it." As for freedom in its individual aspects, he scorned the idea that it could be found in the United States. "I know of no country," he wrote, "in which there is so little independence of mind and real freedom of discussion as in America." This, in his judgment, was why the United States lacked great writers: "There can be no literary genius without freedom of opinion, and freedom of opinion does not exist in America." In one of his most telling phrases, Tocqueville identified the stifling influence as the "tyranny of the majority," which, he said, raised "formidable barriers around the liberty of opinion."[2]

The elegance of Tocqueville's conceptual formulations will always make him, in my opinion, the foremost analyst of American democratic society, but he never did come quite to the point of saying precisely what it was about the American idea of freedom that seemed so anomalous to a European and, more specifically, to a Frenchman. However, his compatriot Michael Chevalier, who also traveled in the United States during the 1830's, did try to distinguish explicitly between French and American conceptions of freedom:

The Yankee type exhibits little variety; all Yankees seem to be cast in the same mold; it was, therefore, very easy for them to organize a system of liberty for themselves. . . . For us, the French, who resemble each other in nothing except in differing from everybody else, for us, to whom variety is as necessary as the air, to whom a life of rules would be a subject of

---

2. *Democracy in America* (Vintage ed., 2 vols.; New York, 1945), I, 56, 273, 274, 275.

horror, the Yankee system would be torture. Their liberty is not the liberty to outrage all that is sacred on earth, to set religion at defiance, to laugh morals to scorn, to undermine the foundations of social order, to mock at all traditions and all received opinions; it is neither the liberty of being a monarchist in a republican country, nor that of sacrificing the honor of the poor man's wife or daughter to one's base passions; it is not even the liberty to enjoy one's wealth by a public display, for public opinion has its sumptuary laws to which all must conform under pain of moral outlawry; nor even that of living in private differently from the rest of the world. The liberty of the Yankee is essentially limited and special like the nature of the race.[3]

Just how serious Chevalier was in asserting the right to seduce a poor man's wife as one of the criteria of freedom in its Gallic form I do not know. But his mere suggestion of it gives us a kind of benchmark that may help define the limits of freedom in its Yankee form. Such behavior would not do at all for Americans, as he recognized, but precisely why? Why does the seduction of a poor man's wife seem more offensive, in American eyes, than the outraging of all that is sacred? The offensiveness, I believe, lies not merely in the violation of morality but also in the violation of equality. For the implication is that Chevalier's kind of freedom would include the right of a rich man to take advantage of a poor man. It was a freedom, in other words, that might be allowed to work in favor of the elite, and as such it was contrary to the American creed. If the rich man were to seduce the wife of another rich man, even Americans of the Victorian age might have regarded the offense as an application of the axiom that all's fair in love and war. But to seduce the

3. *Society, Manners, and Politics in the United States* (Garden City, N.Y., 1961), pp. 327–28.

4

wife of a poor man is to treat a fellow human being as less than equal simply because he is poor. Here the principle of freedom would violate the principle of equality, a consequence perfectly acceptable to the French aristocrat but quite intolerable for a Yankee democrat.

One may say, then, that freedom in the American tradition must meet the negative requirement of not violating the principle of equality. But this still does not identify the distinctive element in the American concept of liberty. Americans have tended to evade the question by defining the word in such unrealistic, all-embracing terms that it is given no meaningful focus. Europeans, in turn, have sometimes suspected that such vagueness is a mask for hypocrisy. Even Bryce got nowhere in a quest for clarification:

I have often asked Americans wherein they consider their freedom superior to that of the English, but have never found them able to indicate a single point in which the individual man is worse off in England as regards either his private civil rights or his general liberty of doing and thinking as he pleases. They generally turn the discussion to social equality, the existence of a monarchy and hereditary titles and so forth—matters which are, of course, quite different from freedom in its proper sense.[4]

Obviously, there is much more involved here than just a difference of definitions, and it is not a question of which is more nearly right—the American or his European critics. The truly interesting problem, instead, is to determine what conditions in American society have convinced Americans that they are the "freest people on earth," and what characteristics of American society have led so many Europeans to conclude that they are not.

4. *American Commonwealth*, II, 635n.

Any answer must no doubt begin with the plain fact that Americans and Europeans have understood freedom in diverse ways. Bryce was perhaps closer than he realized to the heart of the matter when he said that Americans habitually turned the discussion to subjects such as "monarchy and hereditary titles." Now it is unlikely that these people were so simpleminded as to believe, in any literal sense, that an individual's personal freedom depended primarily on whether or not he lived under a monarchical form of government. Their turning of the discussion was actually a somewhat confused attempt to explain what they meant by freedom. They associated certain attitudes with the institution of monarchy and certain other attitudes with a republic headed by a President, who would in time, as it happened, come to exercise more power than most European monarchs.

The essential fact, I believe, is that America had rejected the principle of authority that monarchy symbolized. The visible agency of authority was a ruling class; the operative manifestation of authority was the exercise of coercion on one side and the expression of deference on the other. America, although not a profoundly revolutionary country, had nevertheless rejected this portion of its European heritage. Whatever rule was exercised must be exercised in the name of the people, and no one should be allowed to claim rank as the member of a ruling class. An old American adage asserts that "God and the people hate a chesty man." In short, whatever was done must be done with a maximum of voluntary consent and a minimum of coercion. As for deference, no one owed it to anyone, except perhaps to two classes of people regarded as weak rather than strong—that is, old people and females.

Two familiar phrases emphasize the strongly anti-authoritarian aspect of freedom as it is understood by Americans. One is "free and independent"; the other is "free and equal." The first implies that to avoid dependence, to recognize no higher human authority, is to attain freedom. Great numbers of Americans have construed freedom in exactly this way, attaching only limited value to the right to be different from other people, but attaching immense value to the right not to defer to anyone because of his position. An American newspaper editorial once defined democracy as "the right to curse the cop on the beat." A person would be ill-advised to take this literally, but the danger would not lie in the fact that he had defied authority, for the court would probably be lenient with such an offender. Instead, the risk would lie in the possible reaction of the policeman himself, who, as experience shows, might also defy the authority of the law that forbids him to strike a citizen.

Similarly, the phrase "free and equal" implies that the essence of freedom is not being different from other people, but rather being on a par with other people; not the right to choose between various modes of life, but rather the right to enjoy a mode of life as good as anyone else's. Freedom and equality together constitute a kind of double safeguard against authority; for if all men were free, no one would have an obligation to obey another, and if all were equal, none would have any right to command another. In other words, the principle of freedom assures an individual that no one can control him, not even his superiors, but the principle of equality does even better by assuring him that he has no superiors. America is a land "where every man's a king, and no man wears a crown."

7

In a certain sense, to be sure, equality and freedom are incompatible, for equality implies parity of condition and therefore sameness among individuals, whereas freedom encourages dissimilarity and therefore disparity. A few perceptive Americans have recognized this contradiction, and that brilliant eccentric John Randolph of Roanoke was bold enough to exclaim: "I love liberty; I hate equality."[5] But the Americans to whom I have repeated this aphorism are scarcely even offended by it. They are merely puzzled, finding it extremely difficult to separate liberty from equality. For how can a man without freedom realize the promise that he may be the equal of other men? And if he is equal with others, does not that equality make him immune from being commanded by others, and is not such immunity the essence of freedom? Even Thomas Jefferson, who had a more philosophical understanding of liberty than most Americans, came very close to affirming this equation when he declared it to be self-evident that all men, having been created equal, are for that reason entitled to liberty.

Of course Jefferson, himself an aristocrat of discriminating taste, also understood liberty in the sense of an option to be different, and he would have been as quick as anyone to resist the tyranny of the majority. Many another American, both in the gallery of history and among the plain citizens, has understood it so and defended the right to dissent. Perhaps no words of Ralph Waldo Emerson have been more frequently quoted by his countrymen than the instruction "Whoso would be a man must be a nonconformist." It would be a distortion and an injustice

5. William Cabell Bruce, *John Randolph of Roanoke* (2 vols.; New York, 1922), II, 203.

8

to suggest that freedom of dissent has not been a matter of primary value to many of the best Americans in every generation.

But it does remain true, I believe, that the indiscriminate use of the word freedom has led to a good bit of confusion and has caused some unwary observers to assume that Americans universally subscribed to the idea of liberty as defined by John Stuart Mill—that is, as a guarantee to the individual against being subjected to control by his community. Mill, it will be remembered, insisted that "the only purpose for which power can rightfully be exercised over any member of a civilized community against his will is to prevent harm to others." The exercise of such power for the good of the individual himself is not sufficent warrant. "He cannot be rightfully compelled to do or forbear because it will be better for him to do so, because it will make him happier, because, in the opinion of others, to do so would be wise or even right."[6]

Merely to read Mill's prescription is to realize that this is not the kind of liberty which has prevailed in the United States. Long before the doctrines of the welfare state had begun to press on the latitude of individualism, Americans had already made it clear that they would seek to repress by law any conduct they regarded as immoral or evil, no matter how private this conduct might be. Thus, beginning in 1846, state after state adopted laws prohibiting the manufacture or sale of alcoholic beverages. Not until the second decade of the twentieth century was the Federal Constitution amended to authorize legislation

6. *On Liberty; Representative Government; The Subjection of Women: Three Essays* (World's Classics ed.; London, 1912), p. 15.

making the ban a national one. Prohibition, far from being a temporary aberration, was a movement with a long history in American life.

It is probably in their laws concerning sex and marriage, however, that Americans have most obviously deviated from Mill's formula. For example, the Mormon practice of polygamy was outlawed because it offended the moral sense of the majority, and not because of any demonstration that harm resulted for the individuals who voluntarily adopted the practice. Similarly, in many American states adultery is a crime, no matter how discreetly it may be practiced, whereas in England it has not been criminally punishable for the last three hundred years. Fornication too is no criminal offense in England, but a majority of the American states have statutes providing penalties for fornication under certain conditions. Many states also have laws against various sexual practices even between married persons. The fact that they are seldom enforced does not affect what they reveal about the American concept of freedom.

No less relevant is the large number of states that have laws against interracial marriage, even though they seem incompatible with the principles laid down by the Supreme Court in the famous case of *Brown* v. *Board of Education* (1954). The National Association for the Advancement of Colored People, usually zealous in attacking racially discriminatory legislation, has been conspicuously slow in challenging these miscegenation laws, perhaps from the belief that the American public would take less kindly to judicial rulings that desegregate the marriage bed than to rulings that desegregate the schools. In any case, I venture to predict that when these laws are repealed or invalidated, as they probably will be, the major reason given will not be that they violate freedom, but rather that they violate equality.

Such public regulation of private behavior stands in sharp contrast to the reputation of Americans for hostility—even lawless and violent hostility—to authority of any sort. But the key, perhaps, is the degree to which one person is directly under the control of another. Americans are the most obsessive in their opposition to authority, I believe, when there is a relationship approximating that of ruler and ruled, of commander and subordinate. Power or wealth will be tolerated if the person possessing it takes care to disclaim any pretense of personal superiority. A man may employ servants (which is a matter of function), but he must not put them into livery (which is an assertion of rank). He may attend expensive schools, but he should not speak with too cultivated an accent. He may rise in the world, but he must always lovingly acknowledge his humble origins. If a politically ambitious man lacks humble origins, it will not be amiss for him to invent them. Since all behavior that could be construed as an assertion of superiority is unacceptable, the American people have reserved their heartiest dislike for the officer class in the military, for people with upstage or condescending manners, and for anyone who tries to convert power or influence or wealth into hierarchical ascendancy. In American mores, pulling one's rank has been the unforgivable sin.

This pervasive repugnance for any sort of personal authority has lain close to the heart of the American idea of freedom. It has colored Americans' distrust of power, has encouraged them to diffuse power when they could, and has caused them to shrink from admitting its existence when they could not prevent it from being concentrated. Some of the shortcomings of United States policy in the period since the First World War have resulted, it might be argued, from the fact that Americans have been profoundly reluctant to admit that their country has arrived at a position of power and equally reluctant to shatter their illusion of innocence by accepting the implications and responsibilities of power.

The basic idea of American constitutionalism, of a fundamental document that places limits on government and its officials, was an elaborate effort to depersonalize power and turn the tables, as it were, on the ruling class. The supremacy of the Constitution meant that the rulers would now be ruled—that authority would be disinfected by separating it completely from the personalities of the officials who administered it. The so-called separation of powers was an effort to diffuse authority further by erecting walls between the major departments of government. The Massachusetts constitution of 1780 gave classic expression to the purpose of this device when it declared:

In the government of this Commonwealth the legislative department shall never exercise the executive and judicial powers, or either of them: The executive shall never exercise the legislative and judicial powers, or either of them: The judicial shall never exercise the legislative and executive powers, or either of them: To the end it may be a government of laws and not of men.[7]

Over the years since 1787, the formal separation of powers has suffered considerable erosion as functional ne-

7. Robert J. Taylor, ed., *Massachusetts, Colony to Commonwealth: Documents on the Formation of Its Constitution, 1775–1780* (Chapel Hill, N.C., 1961), p. 131.

cessities have asserted themselves. But the United States has retained the spirit of the principle in a system that makes it almost impossible to initiate any new policy unless all the important interests within the community have given their consent to the change. In spite of all the talk about majority rule, the structure of American politics prevents any majority from carrying out its purposes if significant minorities stand in the way.

More than a century ago, that eloquent defender of minority interests John C. Calhoun made an impressive formal argument for adoption of what he called the principle of the concurrent majority, including a set of two Presidents (one Northern and one Southern) and other devices to assure that the consent of all major interests would be necessary for government action. It is ironical that so many historians have regarded Calhoun's proposal as an antique curiosity in American political thought, for the United States has in fact consistently followed the principle of the concurrent majority.[8]

The massive and unwieldy Federal government is in some ways more notable for its lack of power than for its possession of power. Under the system of unlimited debate in the Senate, which invites occasional use of the extreme practice called filibustering, it is almost impossible for any measure to be enacted if as many as a dozen Senators are determined to resist to the end. In the House of Representatives the Rules Committee has repeatedly blocked the enactment of bills supported both by the administration and by the majority party. Even when a measure has won approval in both houses of Congress,

8. For a more extended treatment of this subject, see David M. Potter, *The South and the Concurrent Majority* (Baton Rouge, La., 1972).

it may run afoul of Presidential veto or invalidation by the Supreme Court. It would, however, require a treatise on government to detail all the features of the constitutional system that work to limit the power of any mere majority and to guarantee that coercive authority will seldom be used to override the wishes of any substantial minority in the United States.

The historical record shows that Americans have habitually displayed a great reluctance to use force—that is, authority in its coercive form—against each other. Instead, they have willingly accepted the instrumentalities that make it possible to defer the unwelcome moment of enforcement—for example, filibusters in Congress, cooling-off periods in labor disputes, and the labyrinthine appellate system that can keep a case in the courts for a decade. In fact, I believe that the marked American reliance on endless discussion as a means of finding solutions for controversies reflects less a faith in the powers of rational persuasion than an unwillingness to let anything reach a point where authority will have to be invoked.

This repugnance for authority need not be illustrated exclusively from the realm of politics, for the same attitude runs through the entire fabric of American life. In the economic sphere, it is by no means clear that Americans have cherished the so-called free-enterprise system because of any real or fancied efficiency that it imparted to the production and distribution of goods. Rather, it seems likely that the competitive market was dear to them because it seemed to do for economic power what written constitutions did for political power. It depersonalized economic power, creating, one might say, an economy of (economic) laws and not of men. Competition also tended to diffuse power, in theory at least, and thus in more ways than one it had the effect of minimizing the visible power of the individual.

Of course, every economic system has employers and employees, or their equivalents, and in these roles there is an almost unavoidable implication of superior and subordinate. But Americans have at least endeavored to soften and blur the relationship when they could not completely deny it. Thus a person who performed the tasks of a servant very often did so without the differentiated manners of a servant and without wearing the special dress of a servant. Also, the use of terms like "hired girl" instead of "maid" and "help" instead of "servants" tended to underline the allegedly voluntary nature of the relationship.

Even those exercising control—the employers and bosses themselves—have rejected the principle of naked authority, and this is perhaps the true measure of its repudiation. Any head of a corporation who finds it necessary to execute his policies by giving categorical orders is likely to regard himself as a failure, for the role the culture assigns him is that of leader rather than commander. He is supposed to enlist the voluntary "cooperation" of his "associates" rather than to demand "obedience" from his "subordinates." Similarly, a President who must actually resort to his constitutional power of veto has in a sense failed as a legislative leader, and a teacher or parent who punishes a child admits defeat in doing so. There is, to be sure, a certain amount of fiction in this view of things, but it is dear enough to those who hold it to encourage their keeping up some pretense of permissiveness on one side and of consent on the other, even when both the permission and the consent are very grudgingly given.

One could go on piling up illustrations, for almost every aspect of American life has reflected this aversion to authority. A dominant theme in American religion, for example, has been the belief that the individual could communicate directly with God, unaided and unimpeded by the intermediation of ecclesiastical authorities. Spiritually, superiors and subordinates do not exist, and the Bible as Holy Writ tends to depersonalize the relationship between God and man, just as a written constitution depersonalizes the relationship between citizen and government, and just as the free market depersonalizes the relationship between wealth and poverty. The basic idea in all cases was that there should be no lords—no lords spiritual, no lords temporal, and no lords economic.

Even in the military establishment, last stronghold of the principle that command shall be unquestioned and obedience unquestioning, the American aversion to authority has manifested itself in many ways. One remembers, for instance, that it took a Prussian officer to instill discipline in the Revolutionary army, and that state militias became a favorite target of ridicule, exemplified in the burlesque slogan "We'll fight till we run, and we'll run till we die." Up to the time of the Civil War, at least, Americans remained incorrigibly civilians, whether in uniform or out. This civilianism eventually gave way, to be sure, under the pressures of modern warfare, but the fundamental hostility to "brass hats" was never dissipated.

American attitudes toward authority are revealed perhaps best of all in the history of changing relationships within the family. Here, as we know, the European heritage, resting on Biblical tradition, was emphatically patriarchal, with a "master of the house" exacting obedience from his wife as well as their children, and with corporal punishment regarded as salutary and essential for discipline. We also know that the American family today is generally considered to be "egalitarian" and American parents "permissive." What needs to be emphasized, however, is that this change began a long time ago. Both Mrs. Trollope and her son Anthony, for example, thought that children in the United States were ungoverned, unpunished, and unattractive. "Can it be, I wonder," mused the latter, "that children are happier when they are made to obey orders and are sent to bed at six o'clock, . . . that an occasional whipping, even, will conduce to rosy cheeks: It is an idea which I should never dare to broach to an American mother."[9] The representative American of that era, it may be worth adding, was a notoriously indulgent parent. When Abraham Lincoln brought his children to the law office he shared with William H. Herndon, it meant that books, legal papers, and furnishings would soon be in disarray, to the intense but suppressed annoyance of his partner. "I have felt many and many a time," Herndon recalled, "that I wanted to wring their little necks, and yet out of respect for Lincoln I kept my mouth shut."[10]

In the older, traditional view, child-rearing resembled the breaking in of a horse, for it required above all the triumph of one will over another. As the nineteenth century wore on, however, parental authority in its coercive form lost much of its respectability. In popular thought the tyrannical father was associated increasingly with the immigrant family and thus with alien influence. Although the spanking of children in the home and in the schools

9. Anthony Trollope, *North America* (New York, 1951), p. 142.
10. J. G. Randall, *Lincoln the President: Springfield to Gettysburg* (2 vols.; New York, 1945), I, 70.

remained common practice throughout the century, it came under considerable attack even before the Civil War. By the 1880's *The Ladies' Home Journal* had launched a veritable crusade against corporal punishment. This was not merely an aspect of the campaign to protect children from physical cruelty, for the worst effects were considered to be psychological. That is, spanking crushed the child's independence, and by destroying the moral relation between parent and child, it had a brutalizing effect on both.[11] Such arguments signalized the gradual repudiation of the authoritarian family, which, as long as it existed, constituted a glaring exception to the peculiarly American ideal of liberty.

An English immigrant writing home in 1818 punctuated his praise of life in America with the crisp remark, "We call no man master here."[12] One of his countrymen struck the same note a century later. D. H. Lawrence, a hostile and often mistaken critic of the United States, was nevertheless deeply perceptive when he said that America meant, above all, being "masterless."[13] But a condition of freedom from overt authority generates its own set of social tensions and psychological needs that are likely sooner or later to require group attention and action. Furthermore, without masters, how does a society get things done? What equivalents does a noncoercive social order put in place of physical force? What inducements to compliance does it substitute for command by superior authority? These questions arise inevitably, for people

11. Daniel R. Miller and Guy E. Swanson, *The Changing American Parent* (New York, 1958), p. 13.

12. Edith Abbott, ed., *Historical Aspects of the Immigration Problem: Selected Documents* (Chicago, 1926), p. 38.

13. *Studies in Classic American Literature* (New York, 1964), p. 8.

will not of their own accord concentrate on social objectives, and if they were to do absolutely what they please all the time, there could be no society at all.

Both for the individual and for society the traditional American rejection of authority left a void that had to be filled somehow. The result, it might be argued, was not to abolish coercion but merely to make it more subtle and impersonal.

CHAPTER TWO

Freedom and Vulnerability

JUST AS HISTORIANS for a long time thought of history as essentially past politics, so they also thought of freedom largely in political terms. That is, freedom meant certain restraints on government, protecting a person against arbitrary arrest, arbitrary seizure of his property, suppression of his views on public affairs, and other such authoritarian treatment. Most of the classic writing on freedom from the time of the ancient Greeks to the present has been in the political context. This was largely the way John Stuart Mill conceived of it in England and Thomas Jefferson in the United States. The incessant boasting about freedom that so annoyed European visitors like Mrs. Trollope and Charles Dickens was nearly always associated with glorification of the American government.

Yet, as we have seen, the American notion of freedom transcended the political realm and in fact extended to every major category of human relationships, including those between employer and employee, clergyman and layman, husband and wife, parent and child, public official and citizen. Americans believed that, as of July 4, 1776, all men were created equal, and that any impairment of a man's equality was destructive of his liberty also.

The distinction between freedom as a mere political status and freedom as a fundamental human condition is a vast one. We know that political freedom can be created whenever a society really wants to create it. This requires a disposition of the majority to exercise some measure of self-restraint, together with certain political devices and arrangements limiting governmental power. But when we consider the nature of man, it is doubtful whether human freedom, in a philosophical sense, can be attained at all. For man is born with needs that will govern him and often even enslave him throughout the whole of his life. In order to live he must eat and drink, and in order to eat and drink he must comply with the terms on which his fellow men are willing to provide food and water. Down through history, these terms have often been onerous ones, but even when relatively mild they have tended to make man something less than completely free.

Man is also the prisoner, in varying degrees, of certain physiological drives, such as sex, and of a number of psychological needs that are partly but not entirely socially created. One of the latter is the need of every human being for some communication with his fellow men. Students of human personality are not sure why this need is so vital. One major factor, a physiological one, is that man must live through a longer period of helplessness than any other creature. During the years of infancy—the very years when his attitudes are forming—the child will die if someone does not take care of him more or less constantly. The possibility of being left alone is a direct and terrible threat to his survival, and the child no doubt senses his dependence in a thousand ways long before that dependence ceases.

But in addition it appears that man has a basic need for a feeling about himself that will give meaning and direction to his existence. This sense of identity is essential to the development of human personality. Without it the mental processes could not be organized and *homo sapiens* would be something less than human. Furthermore, no man can achieve this sense of identity by himself. It is a construct developed from his relations with other human beings. Alone, he cannot orient himself in a universe of overwhelming immensity, but in his relations with others, a realization of their awareness of him helps to steady and focus his awareness of himself. Indeed, it might be said that every person's sense of his own identity is derived from this awareness of other people's perceptions of his identity.

It is in fact a commonplace that man views complete isolation with horror. In the history of crime and punishment, solitary confinement has been dreaded scarcely less than physical torture. Sometimes, if a person has been imprisoned because of his devotion to a cause, he will be sustained by the feeling that he is not alone, even in isolation, because of the unseen companions, perhaps also suffering, who are with him in spirit. But once he becomes convinced that he is truly alone he may swiftly go mad. This was abundantly demonstrated in certain early American prisons where misguided theory led to the widespread use of solitary confinement. Every story of total isolation, such as the adventures of Robinson Crusoe before he found the footprint in the sand, is a veritable horror story. The immense relief that followed the discovery of that footprint, even though it might be the indication of some lurking cannibal, is a measure of the human need for relatedness with other humans. And this need constitutes a further limitation on the possibility of man's achieving complete freedom as an individual.

I have been talking, of course, about the human condition in general, but about aspects of it that have, I believe, been accentuated in the American experience. Thus no other nation has had the same combination of compelling experiences with pioneering, mass immigration, and urbanization—*all* of which tended to intensify the fear of isolation and the feeling of dependence on the group. In addition, it appears that the peculiarly American concept of freedom, overlapping so extensively with the concept of equality, had a similar effect. What this means is that the American may have been becoming psychologically less free at the same time he was becoming institutionally more free, that his disposition to submit to the group may have been increasing at the very time when the formal power of the group to force his submission was decreasing.

But if America has in some respects carried the concept of individual freedom further than most societies, this development is part of a general European tendency that can be traced back at least to the era of the Renaissance and the Protestant Reformation. Before then, in medieval times, the average person was more rigidly fixed in a predetermined social status than he has ever been since. As a peasant, for instance, he might be exploited, but his situation was not in any operative sense a competitive one. He cultivated and disposed of his crops according to fixed rules and settled obligations. Similarly, the craftsman, as a guild member, was regulated in the quantity of his production and the prices he should charge. Scarcely anyone worked in a context of economic rivalry.

In these circumstances, where a man's role was more

or less the same as his identity, where his ties were primary ties, and where there was little of the antagonism and separateness that accompany economic competition, he did not become a fully differentiated individual. His status defined him so completely that it virtually told him who he was. Accordingly, he did not tend to think of himself separately from the social web of his community. He displayed, and probably felt, little desire to discover or assert his "identity" in a subjective sense. He was not, as the psychologists would say, fully individuated.

The child before birth is part of his mother, and after birth remains so intimately related to the mother that he does not develop a sense of separateness until well along in infancy. Full assertion of identity may not occur until after adolescence. Similarly, men in closely integrated communities do not make sharp distinctions between themselves and their kinship groups or fellow villagers.

At some time around the fourteenth and fifteenth centuries, however, certain fundamental changes began noticeably to disturb the tight cohesiveness of medieval life. For one thing, there was an increase in the volume of economic exchange, together with a growth of towns and an expanding use of money as a medium of trade. In this more dynamic economy the regulated production of the guilds was replaced by a new, competitive system of production to meet the growing but fluctuating demands of the market.

These developments tended to destroy the primary ties and reciprocal personal relationships between individuals. In towns, the relative anonymity of the single inhabitant, lost in a mass of other inhabitants, contrasted sharply with the interrelatedness of life in the villages. Men now very often dealt with one another as strangers, and learned to be wary and distrustful in doing so. The system of money exchange destroyed the bond that had once existed between the person who produced something and the person who acquired it. Their relationship became a momentary, automatic transaction, motivated by self-interest on both sides. The growth of unregulated production destroyed the old bonds among guild craftsmen and made them rivals, even antagonists, in a fierce struggle to gain and hold a favorable place in the market. The decline of status liberated men in a greater degree to follow new paths toward fulfillment of their potentialities as individuals, but the decline also meant losing the reassurance of community support.

In short, these developments tended to set men in impersonal and antagonistic relation to one another. They forced each man to realize that he stood apart from other men. If he was a resourceful person, this realization would probably foster his individuality by emancipating him from the network of ties with which society held him in his arbitrarily designated role. It would provide him maximum room for psychological growth and make him, in the fullest sense, a free man. But if he was a weak person, he would probably see such changes, not as presenting him with an opportunity to be free, but rather as threatening him with unbearable insecurity. And there would be a disposition to flee from such a threat by submitting himself to some kind of comforting authority.

Thus the breaking down of the system of primary relationships produced a fundamental dualism, which has been brilliantly analyzed by Erich Fromm.[1] The dilemma presented by this double meaning of freedom is similar

1. *Escape from Freedom* (New York, 1941).

to the one that can be seen in the life of almost any child —on the one hand, the urge to grow up and break free of parental control; on the other, the desperate desire in times of stress to return to the security of an infant's world in which a benevolent parent possessed the power to set the universe right.

Fromm also shows how this dual impulse played itself out in the religious developments of the sixteenth century. Protestantism, in its Lutheran and Calvinistic forms, reflected the emergence of man as an individual by denying the authority of the Church to mediate salvation, and by making each man responsible for seeking his own salvation. Of course this was essentially a recognition of man's freedom and separateness in the realm of religion. But at the same time the new faiths also emphasized the unworthiness of man, the enormity of his sin, and the likelihood of his eternal damnation. Why did they picture God as such a wrathful Jehovah, and why did they insist on the need for man to prostrate himself, stripped and humble, at the feet of this vengeful deity? Fromm believes that such a view of the relation between God and man reflected the fear and the anxiety of men burdened with freedom, that it reflected also their impulse to escape from this anxiety by an intense experience of salvation and to cast off the burden of freedom by submission to a tyrant God.

Anyone who follows Fromm through his full presentation will, I believe, accept his central thesis that the realization of individuality has two aspects, one benign and the other threatening—the aspect of freedom and the aspect of isolation. To put it another way, the burden of isolation is the price man must pay for the blessing of freedom.

Now these things are in a sense as old as humanity. The expulsion of Adam and Eve from the Garden of Eden may be taken as an allegorical representation of the bitter truth that isolation and insecurity are the price of self-knowledge and freedom. Yet the breakdown of the old system of status and the emergence of the free, isolated individual has been a very gradual process extending over centuries, and it has reached a kind of climax in the United States. To be sure, when Fromm wrote *Escape from Freedom* he was especially concerned with Nazi Germany, where the dread of the burden of freedom, he believed, had produced the pathological reaction known as National Socialism. There the impulse toward freedom was obviously overridden by the impulses that led millions to submit themselves unquestioningly to the authority of Der Fuehrer. In America, although the fear of freedom has never yet won a decisive triumph over the impulse toward freedom, the fear has always been present, and we will understand America better if we recognize the continuing struggle between these conflicting impulses.

We will also understand America better if we remember that no other people has been so completely stripped of the psychological support that a system of status provides, and that no other people has had specific historical experiences so likely to accentuate the sense of isolation. Americans, having demanded a higher degree of freedom, have paid a higher price for it in the degree of their psychological isolation. The American insistence on freedom is well known; the price that has been paid for it is less known and deserves some attention.

The basic element in this tension between the quest for freedom and the fear of isolation is the American rejection of status. Status, as we have seen, gave each person a fixed place in the social structure. It assigned each a role and thus assured to each an identity. It did not protect a person against being oppressed, but it did protect him against being lost. Although status systems have deteriorated and undergone modification throughout the Western world during the modern era, American society was probably the first to reject status on principle. Status meant a system of privilege and subservience that even conservative Americans were disposed to repudiate, whether as a matter of conviction or as a matter of policy. Americans have in fact carried this rejection of status to a point where even the least invidious form of subordination is resented as imposing a stigma, and work regarded as menial, even though socially necessary, is seldom performed except grudgingly.

It was ascribed status, not achieved status, that Americans rejected, of course. No one, they believed, should be forced to accept an identity and a role or position in life that were determined by heredity. Yet everyone must have some kind of identity and position, and this meant that Americans had to search for their identities and scramble for positions in the maddest competition this side of the caucus race in *Alice in Wonderland*. The American doctrine of equality did not mean that men were entitled to equal wealth and power. It meant that they should begin as equals in their pursuit of those objectives. Thus American society entered upon a fierce and endless struggle for "upward mobility," with each individual under the constant stress of knowing that he was expected to advance himself as proof of his merit.

It is often regarded as paradoxical, and even as a betrayal of the principle of equality, that Americans should in this way become, in Vance Packard's term, status seekers. But there is really no paradox in the fact that people whose position is indeterminate should be more concerned about defining their position than those whose position is already fixed. And there is no necessary repudiation of equality in the view that a man must justify the gift of equality by making full use of the opportunities it offers him, even if by doing so he goes ahead of someone else.

But this compulsion to improve one's position—that is, to succeed—generates fierce pressures and acute tensions. For many people these tensions are literally not tolerable, and it is a significant fact that some of the most characteristic forms of mental illness in America are those arising from a sense of personal inadequacy and insecurity inspired by a relentlessly competitive system. This is not merely an economic or occupational competition that extends only through a workday. It is also a personal competition, one that includes a felt need to be attractive and popular. It begins when the mother teaches the infant that her love is not entirely unconditional but must be earned by a certain mode of behavior; and it extends from the cradle to the grave.

Of course, the rejection of ascribed status and its consequences are just part of the explanation of psychological isolation in America. The increasing rapidity of social change and the cold impersonality of the modern technological system are other major factors, common enough throughout much of the world. But in addition, as I have suggested, certain distinctive experiences of the American people have tended to accentuate the sense of personal isolation.

To begin with, there was the very act of colonization.

Englishmen left the relative comfort and security of seventeenth-century European civilization to make the lonely, hazardous crossing of a treacherous ocean and settle on the edge of a vast and unknown wilderness. Their pitiful weakness, in contrast with the immensity and savagery of nature, together with the great distance separating them from their homes, must have induced feelings of estrangement too harrowing for us to imagine. In many respects the experience of the early colonists was recapitulated in the experience of nearly three centuries of frontiersmen, as the tide of American settlement rolled westward from the Atlantic to the Pacific. Pioneering was an arduous and often dangerous adventure in which men deliberately isolated themselves and their families from the physical and psychological comforts of civilization. The visual distances of the Great Plains made them perhaps the loneliest part of the American West, especially for women, as poignantly described in O. E. Rolvaag's classic *Giants in the Earth*.[2]

The frontier taught the American pioneer to be self-reliant because it separated him from much of the help usually available from social institutions. To survive, he had to fend for himself—tend his own sick and bury his own dead. The pioneer not only knew that he must spend much time alone but in his backwoods rhetoric often made a virtue of being alone, of living free beyond the sound of the bark of his nearest neighbor's dog. History testifies abundantly to his acceptance of physical isolation, but we get only occasional glimpses of the resulting psychological stresses and their effect on the frontiersman's nature.

2. See also Willa Cather, *My Antonia* (Boston, 1918); and Mari Sandoz's portrait of her father, *Old Jules* (Boston, 1935).

Another relevant experience of major significance in American history was that of the immigrant, who sometimes suffered the torment of being alone in the midst of society, an experience that seems somehow even more desolate than being alone in the wilderness. Of the more than thirty million people who entered the United States as permanent settlers between the 1840's and the 1920's, perhaps two-thirds could speak no English, and many were illiterate even in their native languages. Religion, folk customs, and social outlook also isolated them from the mainstream of American life. Their alternative modes of culture often inspired scorn or anger among native Americans, who in any case habitually excluded the foreigner from their midst without necessarily making a conscious decision to do so. Even worse, immigrants frequently found themselves rejected by their own children, who, having adjusted themselves to the ways of the New World, became ashamed of their parents' speech, behavior, and appearance. It has been demonstrated, for instance, that many second-generation Italians concealed their ability to speak Italian just as they might have concealed a physical defect or the disgrace of illegitimacy. These were the people whom Oscar Handlin called *The Uprooted*. The great majority of them never saw the frontier; yet they knew the meaning of isolation as it was but rarely known in their homelands.

Even native-born Americans of rural origin have suffered the pains of isolation when they moved into the city. Of course their adjustment was usually faster and their ordeal accordingly briefer than that of the immigrant, but to be an identifiable rural alien—that is, a "hick"—in one of the big cities could be, for a time at least, a humiliating and frightening experience. It was a difficult transition from a religious society to a secular one, from a small community rich in personal relations to a depersonalized milieu where one heard few friendly words and soon learned that those one did hear might be bait for a trap. Urban America has disparaged the culture of rural America almost as brutally as it has disparaged the culture of the immigrant. In the words of Andrew Sinclair, "The city eats the bread of the prairie and ignores the source of that bread, while the prairie begins to doubt its own virtue because of the city's indifference and the city's success."[3]

American history has been full of isolating experiences, in the crowded cities as well as on the empty frontier. This isolation, which is in a sense part of the price paid for freedom, has no doubt intensified the insecurities and anxieties of those persons who have been subjected to it. The result often enough is a desperate urge to escape from the uncertainties of independence. The orthodox portrait of the American shows him cherishing and insisting on freedom but seldom indicates the accompanying anxieties that beset him. The Gary Cooper type of American—robust, self-reliant, and buoyant—cannot be a worrier.

It seems possible that this anxiety associated with psychological isolation has been at least partly responsible for certain patterns of behavior often regarded as characteristically American. For instance, an alleged obsession with popularity can perhaps be understood as the American's largely unconscious effort to dispel the chronic apprehension of being alone and an outsider. Then there is also the fact that so many Americans seem to be compulsive workers. They spend excessive amounts of time

3. *Sunday Times* (London), January 27, 1963.

at their jobs, or they hold more than one job. They make work even of their play, and on holiday trips they seem determined that every moment shall be gainfully employed in systematic sightseeing and conscientious photographic recording. For many an American, retirement proves to be traumatic. Although such attitudes are often attributed to the Puritan work ethic, there may be as much desperation as conscience in the urge to keep oneself occupied. The busy person has less time to remember his loneliness. Chaining himself to his work is one path of escape from the sometimes unbearable consequences of freedom.

It need scarcely be said that isolation, whether physical or psychological, may decisively affect the process of maturation; and reciprocally, it should be added, the degree of maturity attained may largely determine how successfully a person can escape from the isolation that is born of freedom. One must be careful, of course, not to infer too much from outward appearances and casual behavior, but there is surely something significant in the frequency with which even relatively sympathetic observers have concluded that Americans as a people are immature. According to the literary critic Leslie Fiedler, for example, immaturity is the key to the shortcomings of American fiction. "Even our best writers," he declares, "appear unable to mature." Their themes belong to "a pre-adult world," and if they live too long "they are likely simply to get worse, ending in intolerable parodies of their own best work." The classic example is Ernest Hemingway, whose "characters seem never really old enough to vote, merely to blow up bridges," and whose controlling values are "a boy's notion of bravery and honor and devotion, tricked out in the child's images of bullfighting and big-game hunting and playing war." The literature reflects the general "regressiveness" of American life—its "implacable nostalgia for the infantile."[4] Thus American men spend much of their leisure time in activities that essentially recapitulate their activities as boys. They do so in part because growing up into isolation has been too painful. Perpetual juvenility, like compulsive industriousness and hunger for popularity, is a route of escape from the distressing consequences of freedom.

The question is whether this urge to escape has become a willingness to surrender—whether the American has freed himself from formal authority only to enthrall himself to other, perhaps more insidious tyrannies.

4. *An End to Innocence: Essays on Culture and Politics* (Boston, 1955), pp. 144, 193.

CHAPTER THREE

Freedom and Conformity

THE UNITED STATES as a superpower in the 1940's and 1950's was obviously a far different nation from the young republic presided over by Thomas Jefferson and Andrew Jackson. Industrialized, urbanized, and in some degree militarized, the American people, according to some analysts, had undergone psychological and social changes of such magnitude as to constitute a veritable transformation of the national character. The "Yankee City" studies of W. Lloyd Warner, for instance, seemed to indicate that social mobility had declined, and that class lines were more consciously and rigidly drawn than in pre-Civil War America.[1]

Meanwhile, David Riesman was discovering a similar historical shift in the way Americans acquired and shaped their fundamental values. His immensely influential book *The Lonely Crowd* distinguished between two basic character structures—the inner-directed man of the nineteenth

1. W. Lloyd Warner and Paul S. Lunt, *The Social Life of a Modern Community* (New Haven, Conn., 1941); Warner and Lunt, *The Status System of a Modern Community* (New Haven, 1942); Warner and Leo Srole, *The Social Systems of American Ethnic Groups* (New Haven, 1945); Warner and J. O. Low, *The Social System of the Modern Factory* (New Haven, 1947); Warner, *The Living and the Dead: A Study of the Symbolic Life of Americans* (New Haven, 1959).

century and the other-directed man of the twentieth century. The behavior of the first sprang from internalized values and commitments fixed relatively early in life and not easily changed by the pressures of circumstance and group opinion. He was thus perpetually stabilized, as it were, by an inner gyroscope. The behavior of the second was governed primarily by the expectations of others. His essential beliefs were sketchy and fluid; he adapted readily to competing values; and he was keenly tuned to all the nuances of attitude among his associates, picking up even faint signals with the sensitivity of a radar screen. In simplified terms, the distinction is between the rugged individualist of the American past and the status-hungry conformist of the American present.

In a great deal of recent fiction and popular nonfiction modern America is pictured as betraying its tradition by becoming more and more socially stratified, class-conscious, and conformist. Novelists such as John P. Marquand and John O'Hara have explored with keen sensitivity the fine, almost invisible gradations of social distinction that make the American social structure an intricate network of half-concealed discriminations. William H. Whyte, Jr., in *The Organization Man* has painstakingly examined the pressures toward conformity that are present in the great corporate bureaucracies of the United States. Vance Packard, in a succession of books with such titles as *The Hidden Persuaders* and *The Status Seekers*, has probably carried to the largest audience the message that America "is undergoing a significant hardening of the arteries of its social system."[2]

2. *The Status Seekers: An Exploration of Class Behavior in America* (New York, 1959), p. 8.

The disillusionment visible in so much of this recent social criticism may well be justified, but it seems to result in some part from certain historical misapprehensions. Perhaps the frontier tradition and the Jeffersonian image of rural America have contributed most emphatically to a widespread impression that the early nation was much closer than the modern one to being a classless society. Yet there is considerable evidence with which to argue that in the nineteenth century discrepancies of wealth were intrinsically greater, class differentiations more meaningful, and patterns of deference certainly more pronounced than they are today. A classless society was never a part of the American experience, and furthermore, it was never cherished as an ideal. On the contrary, social stratification is absolutely essential to the American dream of rising from rags to riches, from log cabin to the White House. Not status itself but change of status is the heart of the matter. Getting ahead, more pedantically called upward social mobility, requires a fair start and the assurance that no level of the social pyramid is sealed off to privilege. Success, viewed as an ascent, would be as impossible in a classless society as in a rigidly stratified one.

If American concern with status is by no means a recent development, the same can be said of American tendencies toward conformism. Riesman, perhaps as a matter of deliberate emphasis, overstates the extent to which the national character has changed since the middle of the nineteenth century. Carl N. Degler seems closer to the mark when he suggests that Riesman's other-directed man sounds very much like Tocqueville's Jacksonian democrat, and that other-directedness has been "the dominant element in our national character through most of our history."[3]

It is indeed Tocqueville, writing about the United States in the 1830's, who provides the classic description of the American as conformist. "It seems at first sight," he wrote, "as if all the minds of the Americans were formed upon one model, so accurately do they follow the same route." The reason was the power of the majority in the United States, which, Tocqueville declared, surpassed all the powers with which Europeans were acquainted.

The authority of a king is physical and controls the actions of men without subduing their will. But the majority possesses a power that is physical and moral at the same time, which acts upon the will as much as upon the actions and represses not only all contest, but all controversy.[4]

Tocqueville, if he did not actually coin the phrase "tyranny of the majority," was apparently the first person to apply it to the United States and certainly far from the last. Lord Bryce, writing a half-century later, concluded that the term was no longer appropriate but discovered a related phenomenon which he called "the fatalism of the multitude." By this he meant the tendency of minorities to submit, not because of coercion by the majority, but rather because of their own democratic conviction that the majority *must* be right. Thus, "out of the mingled feelings that the multitude will prevail and that the multitude, because it will prevail, must be right, there grows a self-distrust, a despondency, a disposition to fall into line, to acquiesce in the dominant opinion, to submit

3. "The Sociologist as Historian: Riesman's *The Lonely Crowd*," *American Quarterly*, XV (1963), 497.

4. *Democracy in America* (Vintage ed., 2 vols.; New York, 1945), I, 273.

thought as well as action to the encompassing power of numbers."[5]

Bryce obviously thought that he was disagreeing with and correcting Tocqueville. To him, "tyranny of the majority" meant the active coercion of minorities by the majority, and this he found to be relatively rare in the United States of the 1880's. But it seems clear that in this instance he misunderstood Tocqueville, who actually used the phrase to mean something very close to Bryce's "fatalism of the multitude." Both men were talking about conformity in the absence of coercion, about submission to the overwhelming psychological force that the majority in a democracy exerts by reason of its very existence.

"Conformity" in a nation that cherishes individualism is bound to be a pejorative word. The modern American as conformist, submitting not only to mass opinion and taste but also to the routinizing influence of machine technology, has become one of the most familiar stereotypes of social criticism. It is often crude caricature, as Max Lerner has said, but "with a core of frightening validity in it." The theme is people mechanized by their material culture:

They spend the days of their years with monotonous regularity in factory, office, and shop, performing routinized operations at regular intervals. They take time out for standardized "coffee breaks" and later a quick standardized lunch, come home at night to eat processed or canned food, and read syndicated columns and comic strips. Dressed in standardized clothes they attend standardized club meetings, church services and socials. They have standardized fun at standardized big-city conventions. They are drafted into standardized armies, and if they escape the death of mechanized warfare they die of highly uni-

---

5. *American Commonwealth* (2 vols.; London, 1888), II, 331.

form diseases, and to the accompaniment of routine platitudes they are buried in standardized graves and celebrated by standardized obituary notices.[6]

The trouble with most stereotypes is not so much what goes into them as what is left out. A conformism that tends to create a spiritual wasteland no doubt deserves all the disdain heaped on it, but such conformism, like many other vices, is in certain respects a virtue carried to excess. It need hardly be said that a certain amount of conformity is essential to the functioning of any social order, but there are some special reasons for emphasizing this fact in respect to the United States.

The making of American nationality did not follow the familiar historical pattern in which smaller political units and ethnic groups are more or less forcibly consolidated. Instead, it resulted from a voluntary drawing together that necessarily included some willingness to conform. Today one has difficulty realizing the many dissimilarities among the American colonies and how much distrust there was, even between neighbors like Massachusetts and Rhode Island, let alone between the thrifty, pious, hardworking folk of New England and the expansive, pleasure-loving plantation lords of the South.

But in the ordeal of the Revolution, the thirteen colonies learned the hard and paradoxical lesson that some sacrifice of individuality was one of the prices of independence. The lesson, moreover, did not cease to be relevant after the victory at Yorktown; for the process of nation-building had barely begun. The tribulations of the post-war years were in part testimony to the disadvantages of excessive nonconformity. It has often been noted that de-

6. *America as a Civilization* (New York, 1957), p. 261.

spite the intense opposition in some states to ratification of the Constitution, there was no challenge to the legitimacy of the government created by the document. The Antifederalists acquiesced in a decision that had gone against them.

We think of majority rule as the central principle of democratic self-government, with guarantees of certain individual rights as the primary and indispensable limitation on that principle. Yet the truly critical element in the democratic process—the one most often weak or absent in democracies that fail—is the readiness of the minority to conform to the will of the majority. Such conformity requires a degree of self-control and public-spiritedness that makes it a severe test of personal and national character. A particularly crucial moment comes when the majority, finding itself converted by the electorate into a minority, must give up ruling for acquiescing. This occurred most notably in 1801, when Federalist acceptance of Thomas Jefferson's victory over the incumbent President, John Adams, marked the first democratic transfer of power in American history. Sixty years later, however, Southern refusal to acquiesce in such a transfer led to civil war and six hundred thousand war deaths.

If the habit of conforming was thus to some extent a functional necessity in the American political system, conformity likewise played its part in the cultural and institutional aspects of nation-building. Here, indeed, progress toward independence seems often to have been inseparable from increases in conformity. For instance, Noah Webster's dictionary and blue-backed speller were expressions of a cultural nationalism aspiring to establish an American language distinctive from that of England. But their effect also was to standardize American usage,

41

and properly so; for a truly "American" language had to be internally uniform as well as externally distinctive.

Similarly, when Frederick Jackson Turner and his disciples spoke of the "Americanizing" influence of the frontier on institutions and character, they had in mind primarily the achievement of differentiation from Europe, but there was also the necessary implication that the frontier had made Americans more like each other. Every allegedly American social invention—such as judicial review, the political party convention, and the manufacturing principle of interchangeable parts—became a national and therefore a truly "American" phenomenon through a process of imitation and conformity that often extended over many decades. The process is especially important in a voluntaristic society with a decentralized political system, and one accordingly finds the pattern repeated endlessly in American history: an innovation, invented or borrowed, catches favor and is imitated enough to become the norm; then the pressure for conformity gradually makes it more or less universal. Such was the case, for example, with the abolition of imprisonment for debt, which began in Kentucky in 1821 and required forty-seven years to prevail in every state.

But if, in the early years, becoming a nation meant becoming something less of a Pennsylvanian or Virginian, with increasing emphasis as the nineteenth century advanced, it also meant becoming something less of an Irishman, German, or Scandinavian. The whole epic of the so-called Americanization of the immigrant is a playing out of the theme of conformity in its most revealing manifestation. Mass immigration, beginning before the Civil War and reaching its peak at the beginning of the twentieth century, converted New York, Chicago, and many other cities into ethnic federations of astonishing variety. The members of each national group tended to cluster in one district, where they maintained their own churches, published their own newspapers in their own language, shopped at their own markets for their own kinds of food, and comforted one another in their poverty and home-sickness as strangers in a strange land.

Public authority did little to discourage the survival of these islands of alien culture. The principal exception, not prevalent until late in the nineteenth century, was state legislation compelling children to attend English-speaking public schools, but to immigrant parents ambitious in their children's behalf such compulsion seemed more of a blessing than a hardship. Otherwise government left their religion undisturbed, their newspapers uncensored, and their customs unsuppressed. It is true that immigrants often felt the hostility of native Americans, but whatever humiliation and injury they may have suffered in this way served only to strengthen further their ethnic solidarity.

Yet despite the strong social and psychological forces holding them together, these enclaves lost much of their distinctiveness by the third generation, and the solvent was conformity. The immigrants had come to America to share in the bounty of American life, and they found it possible to do so fully only if they accepted American ways. Assimilation may be the wrong word to designate what happened, for it suggests the obliteration of Old World values and traits that were often merely adapted or concealed, and it also seems to imply incorrectly that the immigrant's role in the process was largely a passive one. To a considerable extent, in fact, immigrants deliber-ately chose cultural accommodation as the main path to self-improvement.

First-generation immigrants were often too inflexible to travel very far along that path. A great proportion of them lived out their lives in a special kind of loneliness, caught between two cultures, neither of which was entirely real to them. With their children it was usually different. They embraced Americanization willingly and sometimes passionately, but a number of social scientists think they paid a high psychic price in the guilty awareness, however dim, that they had rejected their parents and their heritage. Not until the third generation did both parents and children accept the breaking from tradition as an American tradition itself. In this sense, as Margaret Mead has said, most Americans today are third-generation Americans.[7]

Still, only the immigrant himself was a transitional figure in the sense of having actually lived in two cultures, and his desire to find an American identity may have been all the stronger because of the restraints placed on him by memory, deep-seated habit, and a stubborn accent. There were so many things, big and little, to be changed if he wanted to be recognized by Americans as an American—the pace of his step, the rhythm of his sentences, the angle of his hat, the idiom of his profanity, and the modes in which he expressed pleasure, love, and grief. Sometimes, of course, he became overzealous in his imitation, but such is likely to be the case with proselytes. Those born into an order know which articles of faith are crucial and which are not, but to the newly initiated member every article may seem equally imperative. It is difficult to distinguish the mortal sins from the venial ones.

The experience of the immigrants lends substance to

7. *And Keep Your Powder Dry* (New York, 1942), Chapter III.

Tocqueville's thesis that in America the mass of the people imposed their will on the individual without open coercion but by a kind of irresistible gravitational force:

When the inhabitant of a democratic country compares himself individually with all those about him, he feels with pride that he is the equal of any one of them; but when he comes to survey the totality of his fellows, and to place himself in contrast with so huge a body, he is instantly overwhelmed by the sense of his own insignificance and weakness. The same equality that renders him independent of each of his fellow citizens, taken severally, exposes him alone and unprotected to the influence of the greater number. The public, therefore, among a democratic people has a singular power, which aristocratic nations cannot conceive; for it does not persuade others to its beliefs, but it imposes them and makes them permeate the thinking of everyone by a sort of enormous pressure of the mind of all upon the individual intelligence.[8]

The immigrants, to be sure, were far from surrendering themselves unconditionally to the pressures of Americanization, and Tocqueville surely overstated the extent to which mass opinion crushed independent thought in the age of Jackson, or at any other time. Perhaps the best response to his unflattering analysis, however, is to put conformity in proper perspective. The demeaning connotations of the word tend to obscure the fact that conformity is the necessary corollary of differentiation in the development of group identities. Thus the word American, as I have already suggested, has two fundamental implications. Facing out, it means that the people of the United States are significantly different from the rest of the world's population. Facing in, it means that they are substantially like one another. Similarly at the subna-

8. *Democracy in America*, II, 11.

tional level, when we speak of a teenage culture, we are referring to a phenomenon that combines an often startling distinctiveness with an almost frightening imitativeness. And the fierce conformity of the professional nonconformists of our own day—the "beatniks," for instance —is one of the livelier paradoxes of the age.

The point that seems obvious but has nevertheless been too often overlooked is that American conformity, far from being something extraneous to American freedom, developed integrally along with freedom in a social context of authority rejected and fixed status overthrown. According to Tocqueville's perceptive explication, freedom in America meant primarily the opportunity to improve one's position in life, but the opportunity, to be real, had to be equal for all. Such equality of opportunity could be realized, in turn, only if fixed status were dismantled. But in the presence of true equality no individual dared pit his own beliefs and tastes against those of the mass consensus, and therefore Americans were essentially conformists. In short, freedom meant equality of opportunity, which meant a society without fixed status, which meant that there were not persons sufficiently elite to defy authority, which meant that the individual would comply with the expectations of the majority. One began with freedom and ended with conformity.

Original and perceptive though it may have been, Tocqueville's formulation was essentially theoretical. Noting a strong emphasis on freedom in American expression, while perceiving also, perhaps inaccurately, a preponderant conformity in American behavior, he constructed a brilliant explanation linking the two phenomena. The means of systematic verification were of course unavailable in Tocqueville's time and are probably inad-

46

equate even today. Yet one does find some reinforcement of his thesis in the work of certain modern social scientists. For example, the social psychologist Muzafer Sherif has reported the results of an experiment in which a number of boys at a summer camp were formed into two competitive groups and left to work out their own social rankings and systems of control. One of the behavior patterns observed was the tendency of low-status members to be especially earnest in conforming to the norms of their group, presumably hoping to win recognition in this way.[9] A high-status member of such a group may likewise be strongly motivated toward conformity, for his popularity perhaps depends on it. But it appears that the person of high status may feel freer to depart from group norms if some exterior stimulus should make him wish to do so. Thus a Yale psychologist offers the hypothesis, admittedly difficult to test, that "the more highly a person is valued by the other members the more tolerance will be shown his deviations from the group norms and therefore the greater freedom he will feel in accepting communications contrary to them. In other words, the higher the person's social rank in the group, the less will be his anxiety concerning nonconformity."[10] One study of a group of industrial laborers, for instance, revealed that production norms imposed rigorously on newcomers were relaxed in the case of well-established workers, whose infractions, by contrast, went largely unpunished. Here "the degree of conformity required of a member

9. "A Preliminary Experimental Study of Inter-Group Relations," in John H. Rohrer and Muzafer Sherif, eds., *Social Psychology at the Crossroads* (New York, 1951), pp. 388–424, especially p. 420.

10. Carl I. Hovland et al., *Communication and Persuasion* (New Haven, Conn., 1953), p. 150.

appeared to be inversely related to the extent to which he was accepted by the others."[11]

These and other plodding experiments in tracks left by Tocqueville's intuition more than a century ago are far from conclusive, but they do tend to reinforce the impression that a man who is unsure of his social status will be more likely to do what others are doing, to believe what others tell him to believe, and even to anticipate what the group expects of him without being told at all.

It appears, then, as an ironical example of the law of compensation that persons relatively free of status may be less free in their ideas than those whose status is relatively fixed; and it also appears that persons who cannot be commanded may be more amenable to persuasion than those who would respond to command. But every society, to survive, must somehow coordinate the work of its members. Where authority and coercion have been displaced there must be control without command through persuasion of an often subtle and indirect kind. As Erich Fromm has written, members of such a society "have to *desire* what objectively is *necessary* for them to do. *Outer force* is to be replaced by *inner compulsion* and by the particular kind of human energy which is channeled into character traits."[12] Thus social control in a voluntaristic society is less a matter of regulating behavior than of shaping attitudes and character, and that is a far more complex enterprise, requiring a more profound understanding of human nature.

11. *Ibid.*, p. 151.
12. "Individual and Social Origins of Neurosis," in Clyde Kluck-hohn and Henry A. Murray, eds., *Personality in Nature, Society, and Culture* (New York, 1949), p. 409.

CHAPTER FOUR

Noncoercive Control

ONE WAY of defining the American political experiment inaugurated in 1776 would be to say it rested on the assumption that a free society was one in which men applied a minimum of force to each other. Americans on the eve of the Revolution were especially concerned about various instrumentalities of force—such as arbitrary arrest, trial without jury under admiralty law, the presence of a standing army, and of course the imposition of taxes without public consent. In erecting their own new structures of government, they accordingly took great pains to limit the coercive power of officials and set up constitutional bulwarks against arbitrary force, believing that to cage such force was to make freedom secure.

This was a noble dream and at the same time a realistic judgment on human history, with its endless record of forcible exploitation and oppression. Still, it reflected a somewhat naïve conception of the nature of power and freedom, placing too much emphasis on social control as exclusively a matter of applying naked force. It is important to distinguish between force and power, as many political thinkers of modern times have endeavored to do. Force or coercion is one technique for achieving a purpose. Power is not a technique but rather the capacity to achieve a purpose. It may be defined, says Bertrand Russell, as the "ability to cause people to act as we wish when they would have acted otherwise but for the effects of our desires."[1] Similarly, R. H. Tawney defines power as "the capacity of an individual or group of individuals to modify the conduct of other individuals or groups."[2] Now, such modification of behavior may be achieved by direct physical coercion or by the threat of coercion. One could point to chattel slavery and the hickory-stick mode of child-rearing as examples out of the American past. Nevertheless, coercion is far from typical. "It cannot be concluded . . . as many have," says Charles E. Merriam, "that the essence of the power situation is force in the sense of violence."[3]

The alternatives to coercion that are operative in any society constitute significant reflections of its fundamental character, and of course they are subject to the shifting influences of historical change. "The foundations of power," Tawney declares, "vary from age to age, with the interests which move men, and the aspects of life to which they attach a preponderant importance. It has had its source in religion, in military prowess and prestige, in the strength of professional organization, in the exclusive control of certain forms of knowledge and skill, such as those of the magician, the medicine man, and the lawyer."[4] Certainly throughout most of American history the application of physical force has been less significant than other means of social control, such as the exclusive possession

1. *The Prospects of Industrial Society* (New York, 1923), p. 190.
2. *Equality* (New York, 1931), p. 230.
3. *Political Power, Its Composition and Incidence* (New York, 1934), p. 20.
4. *Equality*, pp. 230–31.

of a charter or patent or strategic piece of ground that serves the needs of a considerable number of people. Power, in other words, often consists simply in the ability to withhold something that is generally needed, and this means in turn that only a fraction of the control exercised over the daily lives of individuals is public control through law. The historian and sociologist Harry Elmer Barnes once estimated that fraction as less than one-tenth.[5]

If power and control are something more than the application of force, then freedom must consist of something more than immunity from the application of force. And if that is true, then the concept of freedom embraced by the Founding Fathers was too limited. A broader definition would take into account the limitations of freedom achieved by the exploitation of needs. In such terms, the principal diagnostic feature of freedom might well be a condition in which needs are either reduced to a minimum or somehow rendered unexploitable. To construe freedom in this way is to recommend a fundamental reworking of the whole history of freedom in America— a history usually written as a record of the restraints placed on coercive power.

Americans have in fact been too ready to believe that the "blessings of liberty" are political blessings. They have even supposed that they could spread freedom around the globe by encouraging democratic elections, representative legislatures, guarantees of civil rights, and the other familiar features of their own political system. Yet perhaps the most important functional condition of American freedom was the escape the North American continent provided from the land monopolies of the Old World. To

5. *Sociology and Political Theory* (New York, 1924), p. 6.

say this is to put the problem of freedom in a context of needs rather than of laws. Men needed to eat, and before the Industrial Revolution this meant that they needed land upon which to grow food. In the Old World, where land was scarce in proportion to the population, landlords exercised so much power over their tenants that the latter could not be regarded as truly free men. But in America the great abundance of land frustrated repeated efforts to set up systems of social control based on the old European scarcity of land. As a consequence the American people became, to a considerable degree, a nation of landowners, and perhaps in this sense they had good reason to boast of being "the freest people on earth."

But if Americans were ever willing to be satisfied with bread from their own grain and meat from their own animals—which is exceedingly doubtful—they did not remain satisfied for long. They might enshrine agrarian man, the subsistence farmer, as the symbol of rustic republican virtues, but for themselves they wanted cash income, which they could get only by going to market. Here, then, was a new complex of needs—for transportation, seasonal and long-term credit, adequate markets, and more sophisticated agricultural equipment. These needs gave power to the railroad company, the banker, the grain merchant, and the manufacturer of farm machinery, and in proportion as these needs tightened upon them, farmers began to feel progressively less free. The great Populist movement of the late nineteenth century was fundamentally an expression of the awareness of grain farmers in the West and cotton farmers in the South that they were losing their freedom.

Furthermore, as the complex industrial economy of the modern age developed, an increasing number of men felt the pressure of another imperative need—the need for employment. Factory production replaced much of the old craft production, and access to factory machinery, as Karl Marx so clearly perceived, became vital to the livelihood of the worker. The wage earner lost much of his freedom vis-à-vis the industrial proprietor, and many social critics expected him to end by losing it all. But the degree of his dependence varied with the extent to which alternative employment was available. Without any alternative opportunity, the worker could be forced to labor for a bare subsistence, and he became in a real sense a man without freedom, a wage slave. If other employment were available, the worker could in a sense negotiate for the sale of his labor. Of course he still had a vital need for a wage, but no one person could exploit his need, and to that extent he was free. It appears that in the United States, as compared with other industrializing nations of the nineteenth century, alternative employment opportunities were somewhat more available; for the ratio of natural resources to population was high, and the geographic expansion of the nation continually created new centers of industrial activity.

If it is valid thus to measure freedom partly in terms of the extent to which the things men need are controlled by others, and if the emphasis is placed primarily on the physical need for food, clothing, shelter, and the money with which to buy them, then it might appear that Americans, as they moved into the twentieth century, were becoming less free. After the Civil War a much higher percentage of them had become employees, dependent on others for a livelihood. The prevalence of sweated labor conditions, the relative weakness of organized labor, and the special vulnerability of the new masses of immigrants all contributed to a general decline in available alternatives for a large part of the population. A change got under way in the 1930's, however. Organized labor grew stronger; racial exclusion and other barriers to opportunity began to crumble; technology opened great new ranges of employment; and the resulting increase in mobility seemed to signify a trend toward increased freedom once more.

Yet such an interpretation of recent tendencies in the history of freedom probably depends too narrowly on consideration of the power relationship between employer and employee. There was a time, to be sure, when increases in production appeared to be the sole end of economic activity, and when exploitation of labor was a primary means of securing those increases. But in modern American society the role of the individual as a consumer is no less important than his role as a producer, and the devices with which the consumer may be controlled are of an entirely different order from the power linkage between worker and employer.

To this one must add the obvious fact that many of the needs by which man may be controlled are noneconomic. In the United States especially, as we have seen, escape from the coziness of a status-bound society has produced a need for psychic equivalents of status to counteract the loneliness and uncertainty of excessively individualized freedom. The yearning to know where one stands has expressed itself in a variety of ways, such as Ahab's compulsion to hunt down the White Whale and Thomas Wolfe's Faustian longing to range through the entire universe of human knowledge and experience. But perhaps the most characteristic mode of self-definition in America has been the quest for "success." The hunger for success may be seen as an effort to fill the psychological void left by the rejection of status. Since status is a position assigned by others, success, as the surrogate for status, had to be defined in terms universally recognizable. The one common denominator of achievement that everyone could understand was money; and so money, the modern means by which physical needs are satisfied, became also the symbol of success, fulfilling an urgent psychic need. Americans, as a consequence, acquired a reputation for materialism not entirely deserved.

Yet the acquisition of wealth was the mere threshold of success, American style, which depended also on the degree of respect with which a person was viewed in his social milieu. To some extent this respect could be bought with money, but it did not come automatically with the possession of money. There was the further need to win the approval of society as the ultimate mark of success. Now this compulsion to succeed did not limit the freedom of the nineteenth-century American in the sense of making him subject to the power of any one person. Men were then on the whole more exploitable in their need for a living wage than in their psychic needs; for the power relationship between employer and employee was relatively direct and simple, while the struggle for self-realization and success was a disorderly affair, subject to little control except that of the marketplace and public opinion. But in the modern American context of automated production and material abundance, a person's role as a consumer is less predictable and therefore more critical than his role as a producer. From year to year American taste in automobile-buying has a greater effect on the national economy than the periodic strikes in the automobile industry. At the level of physical needs, therefore, the principal effort at control is directed toward influencing what people buy and, indeed, sometimes inducing them to buy more than they should.

Such control over people as consumers is much different, of course, from the old controls over people as producers. It means arranging somehow that a person shall want and choose to do what one wants him to do, rather than ordering or compelling the action desired of him. It therefore depends almost entirely on persuasion or something resembling persuasion. It involves the exercise of power without coercion, directed at a man's total personality and reaching him through his psychic as well as his physical needs. It in fact requires a calculated and often subtle effort to induce the kind of willing conformity that in Tocqueville's time seemed to result primarily from the involuntary force of mass opinion.

Control exercised by means of persuasive and manipulative attention to another person's physical and psychic needs may require a degree of indirection that seems to border on deception. But it does not necessarily constitute exploitation, which is the use of power for the benefit of the user and to the detriment of the person over whom the power is exerted. Within the institutions of the family and public education, for instance, modern Americans have replaced much of the older kind of discipline with a more delicate, manipulative mode of control. A good deal of what has been labeled permissiveness is really an effort at gentler and subtler control, one that has brought children at last within the purview of the long-standing American repugnance for naked authority. Whatever disagreement there may be about the effect of such methods on the building of character, they can scarcely be considered exploitative in purpose or effect.

It is a different matter, however, when one studies the institution that most faithfully reflects the revolutionary emergence of a consumer society. I refer to the institution of modern advertising.

The transformation from a nation preoccupied with modes of production to a nation whose social character is embodied primarily in its modes of consumption was bound to mean an increase in the power of the advertising complex. Indeed, it is difficult here to separate cause from effect, for advertising obviously helped produce that transformation. But the modern significance of advertising goes far beyond its great influence on the buying habits of a consumer society. The crucial consideration is the extent to which the ends and means of advertising have come to dominate mass communication generally in the United States.

Even those older media of mass communication, newspapers and magazines, have become increasingly dependent on advertising for their existence. Readers still pay part of the total cost of publication, but a relatively small part, and circulation figures are primarily important for the advertising they will attract. Thus a newspaper's social function is to provide the public with information, but its survival function is to sell advertising.

It was with the emergence of radio and television, however, that the advertising industry entered fully into its modern role as one of the principal agencies of social control. For one thing, with the exception of a few subscription stations, these new media are totally financed from the sale of advertising, and there is far more sponsor control of programming than there ever was dictation of newspaper policy by advertising patrons.

Even more important is the nature of the new media

and the way in which they affect their mass audience. The sound of human speech and the sight of human expression carry an impact difficult to equal using just the printed word. The emotional power of radio was demonstrated by Adolf Hitler, Winston Churchill, and Franklin Roosevelt in the dramatic setting of the Second World War. The emotional power of television is even greater, though it has yet to be measured with any degree of comprehensiveness and accuracy. Meanwhile, it seems clear enough that these new media are less rational instruments of communication than the older ones. Furthermore, we have brought radio and television into the intimate places of our lives—to our living rooms, bedrooms, and nurseries—giving the voices of strangers an access to our privacy that we would never think of giving to a salesman in person. What all this reduces to is that most of the communications received by the American people outside of their schools are not paid for by themselves or their government, but rather are financed and controlled by parties who have ulterior motives in sending them. It seems likely that this condition, prevailing over a substantial period of time, would of itself have a significant effect on the American character.

The egregious features of American advertising have been catalogued and anathematized often enough, sometimes at a level of sensationalism that few advertisers themselves ever attain. It scarcely needs to be said that advertising is in no small degree a modern necessity, and that some of it is eminently informative and responsible. That it too often tends to degrade standards of taste and even standards of morality may well be true, but my interest here is principally in advertising as an agency of social control affecting the quality of American freedom.

Advertising is exploitative to the extent that it induces people to act against their own best interests. Since rational argument cannot ordinarily persuade one so to act, the appeal must be an irrational one; and since men are likely to reject irrational appeals if they recognize them as such, the irrationality, to succeed, must be camouflaged.

Television in the United States has proved to be a highly effective medium for indirect and covert appeals to the irrational side of man's nature. In the first place, the viewer tunes in to watch the program and absorbs the accompanying advertiser's message without giving it much deliberate attention. The exploitation begins with the programming, for though the ultimate purpose of commercial television is to sell goods and services, the preliminary and equally essential purpose is to maximize the number of viewers. Network competition for the prime-time audience has become a cutthroat affair in which aesthetic quality occasionally triumphs but more often yields, not to the average taste of the multitude, but to the lowest taste of the multitude.

The despotic rule of ratings in American television programming would no doubt be recognizable to Tocqueville as a new manifestation of his "tyranny of the majority," but in this case it is a manipulated majority. Among the various means of seizing and holding the attention of millions of viewers week after week, one might mention the high frequency of scenes depicting physical violence, which, unlike erotic themes, appear to be largely immune from the censor's pencil, and the popularity of the open-ended series, which sooner or later becomes a cliché but has the commercial advantage of being habit-forming. Within the limits set for them, television artists usually do their professional best to entertain and sometimes to uplift the television audience, but the measure of their success is the total number of people they can tempt into watching the commercials, and in that sense they, as well as the advertisers, are engaged in exploitation.

The exploitative nature of the advertising itself, though frequently noted, is perhaps generally regarded as the price that must be paid for an immense amount of inexpensive entertainment. Commercials, as a matter of common practice, stimulate the purchase of things the viewer may not physically need by exploiting his or her psychic needs and fears—such as the need to feel successful or masculine or beautiful, such as the fear of ill health or of growing old or of having bad breath. Thus the sponsor's product is often sold by peddling dreams and remedies for nightmares. The transactions are not very different from those of the primitive medicine man who had special knowledge both of the anger of the gods and of how to propitiate them. Psychological manipulation is nothing new, but television has given it tremendous amplification and unprecedented mass effect.

Modern advertising, as I have said elsewhere, wields an immense social influence, comparable to the influence of religion and education. Yet it has no social goals and no social responsibility for what it does with its influence, so long as it refrains from palpable violations of truth and decency.[6] The power of advertising, as we have seen, extends beyond the control exercised over patterns of consumption to the financial domination of all the major media of mass communication. But beyond even that, one

6. David M. Potter, *People of Plenty: Economic Abundance and the American Character* (Chicago, 1954), p. 177.

must take into account the extent to which the techniques of advertising have been adopted in other social realms, such as education, religion, and politics. The careful "packaging" of political candidates for the purpose of synthesizing a "public image" is a more serious matter than the television commercial designed to exploit unfulfilled desires, for it is one thing to persuade a man to buy the wrong automobile and something else again to persuade him to vote for the wrong Presidential candidate.

Television seems to be the best example and aptest symbol of all the manipulative forces brought to bear daily on the consciousness and subconsciousness of the modern American in his voluntaristic society. He is, after all, perfectly free to turn that knob or dial and yet has in a way been programmed not to do so. This does not mean that his sense of being free is an utter illusion, and that he has been victimized by a gigantic conspiracy to brainwash him. It does appear, however, that the modern American, still thinking of freedom in the old-fashioned way as independence from coercive authority, may very well overestimate the extent to which he is free. In fact, compared with the Negro slave and exploited factory worker of the nineteenth century, he probably has a relatively unclear idea of how his freedom is limited. Perhaps what all this means is that freedom for the modern American depends less than ever before on resistance to the controls exerted by others and more than ever on his own willpower and self-control. Eternal vigilance remains the price of liberty, but the first person to watch is oneself.

Bibliography

Bibliography of the
Published Works of David M. Potter

Compiled by George Harmon Knoles

T HIS COMPILATION was developed from a number of
sources, including records left by David Potter, search-
es in the major journals to which he contributed articles
and book reviews, and information supplied by publishers
and former colleagues. Despite my efforts to achieve com-
pleteness, I can only hope—not assert—that I have found
everything of importance he published. With the exception of a very few items—fewer than ten—I was able to
check the information gathered with the publications
themselves. In addition to the Bibliography proper, I have
included lists of the major reviews of the books written
or edited by David Potter. The list for the last one, *The
Impending Crisis, 1848–1861*, is necessarily incomplete,
for that book, completed by Don E. Fehrenbacher, was
published less than a year before this Bibliography was
set in type. Finally, I have appended a list of essays and
obituaries on David Potter the man and the historian.

In general, I list the items chronologically, believing
that this ordering would prove useful to those interested
in following David Potter's intellectual development. Reviews of his books and the publishing history of his works
have been subordinated typographically to the listings in
the Bibliography proper, thus substantially preserving the
chronological arrangement of the whole.

A number of persons were helpful in providing information for this project. I owe a debt of gratitude to Thomas A. Bailey, Barton J. Bernstein, Carl N. Degler, Don E. Fehrenbacher, and David M. Kennedy, Professor Potter's colleagues in the Stanford Department of History, for their interest and assistance. Others who contributed data for which I am appreciative are Jim Barnett, Editorial Assistant, Yale University Press; Ann Barret, Assistant to the Director, the University of Chicago Press; Virgil Hartley, former Managing Editor, *The Emory University Quarterly*; Howard R. Lamar, Department of History, Yale University; Akihiko Nakazato, Center for American Studies, University of Tokyo; and Otis Pease, Department of History, University of Washington. Finally, I wish to thank the Institute of American History at Stanford and its secretary, Betty Eldon, for office assistance in compiling this Bibliography.

GHK

The Published Works of David M. Potter

1932
"The Rise of the Plantation System in Georgia," *Georgia Historical Quarterly*, XVI (June 1932), 114–35.

1934
"A Bibliography of the Printed Writings of Ulrich Bonnell Phillips," *Georgia Historical Quarterly*, XVIII (September 1934), 270–82.

1940
Review of *Jonathan Edwards, 1703–1758: A Biography*, by Ola Elizabeth Winslow (New York: Macmillan, 1940); *Ethan Allen*, by Stewart H. Holbrook (New York: Macmillan, 1940); *Daniel Boone*, by John Bakeless (New York: William Morrow, 1939); *Old Tippecanoe: William Henry Harrison and His Time*, by Freeman Cleaves (New York: Scribner's, 1939); and *Fremont: Pathmarker of the West*, by Allan Nevins (New York: Appleton-Century, 1939), *The Yale Review*, XXX (September 1940), 174–79.

1941

"Horace Greeley and Peaceable Secession," *Journal of Southern History*, VII (May 1941), 145–59.

> Reprinted in *The South and the Sectional Conflict* (1968), pp. 219–42.

Review of *Lincoln Takes Command*, by John Shipley Tilley (Chapel Hill: University of North Carolina Press, 1941), *Journal of Southern History*, VII (August 1941), 410–11.

1942

Lincoln and His Party in the Secession Crisis (New Haven, Conn.: Yale University Press, 1942). Yale Historical Publications, Studies 13.

> Republished as a Yale Paperbound, 1962. Chapter 12 reprinted in Edward Wagenknecht, ed., *Abraham Lincoln, His Life, Work, and Character* (New York: Creative Age Press, 1947), pp. 319–31. Materials from throughout the book reprinted in Norton Garfield, ed., *Lincoln and the Coming of the Civil War* (Boston: Heath, 1959), pp. 60–69.

> Reviewed by Thomas Robson Hay, *New York Times Book Review*, September 27, 1942, p. 5; Margaret Leech, *The Nation*, October 31, 1942, pp. 454–55; Kenneth M. Stampp, *Mississippi Valley Historical Review*, XXIX (December 1942), 438–39; T. Harry Williams, *American Political Science Review*, XXXVI (December 1942), 1187; Howard C. Perkins, *Journal of Southern History*, IX (February 1943), 124–25; and Wood Gray, *American Historical Review*, XLVIII (April 1943), 591–92.

Review of *Justice in Grey: A History of the Judicial System of the Confederate States of America*, by William M. Robinson, Jr. (Cambridge, Mass.: Harvard University Press, 1941), *Texas Law Review*, XX (January 1942), 393–96.

1943

Review of *The Life of Johnny Reb: The Common Soldier of the Confederacy*, by Bell I. Wiley (Indianapolis: Bobbs-Merrill, 1943); and *Our Soldiers Speak, 1775–1918*, by William Matthews and Dixon Wecter (Boston: Little, Brown, 1943), *The Yale Review*, XXXII (June 1943), 824–27.

Review of *Lincoln and the Patronage,* by Harry J. Carman and Reinhard H. Luthin (New York: Columbia University Press, 1943), *Journal of Southern History,* IX (November 1943), 575–77.

Review of *Origins of the American Revolution,* by John C. Miller (Boston: Little, Brown, 1943), *The Yale Review,* XXXIII (December 1943), 370–71.

1944

"Huey Pierce Long," in *Dictionary of American Biography,* Supplement I (1944), pp. 506–8.

Review of *Lee's Lieutenants: A Study in Command,* Vol. III, by Douglas Southall Freeman (New York: Scribner's, 1944), *The Yale Review,* XXXIV (December 1944), 360–62.

> Reprinted in John Albert Sanford, ed., *A College Book of Prose* (Boston: Ginn, 1947), pp. 462–63.

1945

Edited *Trail to California: The Overland Journal of Vincent Geiger and Wakeman Bryarly* (New Haven, Conn.: Yale University Press, 1945). Yale Historical Publications, Manuscripts and Edited Texts 20.

> Republished as a Yale Western Americana Paperbound, 1962.
>
> Reviewed by Keith Hutchison, *The Nation,* January 19, 1946, p. 83; John Weld, *New York Times Book Review,* January 20, 1946, p. 26; Fletcher M. Green, *Emory University Quarterly,* II (March 1946), 62–63; Walker D. Wyman, *Mississippi Valley Historical Review,* XXXII (March 1946), 624–25; Herbert O. Brayer, *Journal of Southern History,* XII (May 1946), 279–80; Irene D. Paden, *Pacific Historical Review,* XV (June 1946), 230–31; and Ralph P. Bieber, *American Historical Review,* LII (July 1947), 749–51.

"The Jackson Collection of Lincolniana," *Yale University Library Gazette,* XIX (1945), 22–28.

Review of *The Young Jefferson, 1743–1789,* by Claude G. Bowers (Boston: Houghton Mifflin, 1945), *The Yale Review,* XXXIV (June 1945), 738–40.

Review of *The Wilson Era: Years of Peace, 1910–1917,* by Josephus Daniels (Chapel Hill: University of North Carolina Press, 1944); *Woodrow Wilson and the Great Betrayal,* by

Thomas A. Bailey (New York: Macmillan, 1945); and *Woodrow Wilson and the People,* by H. C. F. Bell (New York: Doubleday, Doran, 1945), *The Yale Review,* XXXV (September 1945), 161–64.

1946

Review of *Mr. Lincoln's Camera Man: Matthew B. Brady,* by Roy Meredith (New York: Scribner's, 1946); *The Beleaguered City: Richmond, 1861–1865,* by Alfred Hoyt Bill (New York: Knopf, 1946); and *A Volunteer's Adventures: A Union Captain's Record of the Civil War,* by John William DeForest, edited by James H. Croushore (New Haven, Conn.: Yale University Press, 1946), *The Yale Review,* XXXV (June 1946), 733–36.

Review of *Lincoln and the South,* by James G. Randall (Baton Rouge: Louisiana State University Press, 1946), *Journal of Southern History,* XII (August 1946), 441–42.

Review of *American Radicalism, 1865–1901: Essays and Documents,* by Chester McA. Destler (New London: Connecticut College, 1946), *New England Social Studies Bulletin,* IV (September 1946).

Review of *Alexander H. Stephens: A Biography,* by Rudolph von Abele (New York: Knopf, 1946), *The Yale Review,* XXXVI (December 1946), 356–58.

1947

"The Historical Development of Eastern–Southern Freight Rate Relationships," *Law and Contemporary Problems,* XII (Summer 1947), 416–48.

> Reprinted without statistical charts in Richard M. Abrams and Lawrence W. Levine, eds., *The Shaping of Twentieth-Century America: Interpretive Articles* (Boston: Little, Brown, 1965), pp. 26–61.

Review of *Autographs: A Key to Collecting,* by Mary A. Benjamin (New York: Bowker, 1946), *Papers of the Bibliographical Society of America,* XLI (First Quarter), 61–63.

Review of *A Benjamin Franklin Reader,* edited by Nathan G. Goodman (New York: Thomas Y. Crowell, 1946), *William and Mary Quarterly,* IV (January 1947), 106–9.

Review of *The Diary of a Public Man and a Page of Political*

Correspondence, Stanton to Buchanan, edited by F. Lauriston Bullard (New Brunswick, N.J.: Rutgers University Press, 1946), *Journal of Southern History*, XIII (February 1947), 118–19.

Review of *Lincoln's War Cabinet*, by Burton J. Hendrick (Boston: Little, Brown, 1946); *Thurlow Weed: Wizard of the Lobby*, by Glyndon G. Van Deusen (Boston: Little, Brown, 1947); and *The Diary of a Public Man and a Page of Political Correspondence, Stanton to Buchanan*, edited by F. Lauriston Bullard (New Brunswick, N.J.: Rutgers University Press, 1946), *The Yale Review*, XXXVI (March 1947), 549–52.

Review of *King Linkum the First: A Musical Burletta Performed at the Concert Hall, Augusta, Georgia, February 23, 1863*, by John Hill Hewitt, edited by Richard B. Harwell (Atlanta: Emory University Library, 1947), *Emory University Quarterly*, III (June 1947), 124–25.

Review of *The Lincoln Reader*, edited by Paul M. Angle (New Brunswick, N.J.: Rutgers University Press, 1947), *Mississippi Valley Historical Review*, XXXIV (June 1947), 131–32.

Review of *Experiment in Rebellion*, by Clifford Dowdey (Garden City, N.Y.: Doubleday, 1946), *American Historical Review*, LII (July 1947), 752–53.

Review of *The Shaping of the American Tradition*, 2 vols., edited by Louis M. Hacker and Helene S. Zahler (New York: Columbia University Press, 1947), *The Yale Review*, XXXVII (September 1947), 174–76.

1948

Co-edited with James H. Croushore, *A Union Officer in the Reconstruction*, by John William DeForest (New Haven, Conn.: Yale University Press, 1948).

> Reviewed by Avery Craven, *New York Herald Tribune Book Review*, June 13, 1948, p. 2; Lloyd Lewis, *New York Times Book Review*, July 18, 1948, p. 19; Perry Miller, *New England Quarterly*, XXI (September 1948), 392–94; Harris E. Starr, *American Historical Review*, LIV (October 1948), 214; and T. Harry Williams, *Journal of Southern History*, XIV (November 1948), 560–61.

The Lincoln Theme and American National Historiography: An Inaugural Lecture Delivered Before the University of Oxford on 19 November 1947 (Oxford: Clarendon Press, 1948).

Reprinted in *The South and the Sectional Conflict* (1968), pp. 151–76.

"The Marshall Plan and American Foreign Policy," *Current Affairs* (London), February 21, 1948, pp. 5–18.

"The Future of the Negro in the United States," *The Listener* (London), July 15, 1948, pp. 85–86, 97.

> Abridged and reprinted as "A Happier Path for American Negroes?," *The English Digest*, XXIX (November 1948), 73–76.

Review of *Horace Greeley and the Republican Party, 1853–1861: A Study of the New York Tribune,* by Jeter Allen Isely (Princeton, N.J.: Princeton University Press, 1947), *American Historical Review,* LIII (January 1948), 358.

Review of *Rebel Raider: Being an Account of Raphael Semmes's Cruise in the C.S.S. Sumter Composed in Large Part of Extracts from Semmes's Memoirs of Service Afloat, Written in the Year 1869,* selected and supplemented by Harpur Allen Gosnell (Chapel Hill: University of North Carolina Press, 1948), *Mississippi Valley Historical Review,* XXXV (December 1948), 521–22.

1949

Co-edited with Thomas G. Manning, *Nationalism and Sectionalism in America, 1775–1877: Select Problems in Historical Interpretation* (New York: Henry Holt, 1949).

> Reviewed by Richard W. Leopold, *William and Mary Quarterly,* VII (April 1950), 324–26; and Robert W. Iversen, *Mississippi Valley Historical Review,* XXXVII (September 1950), 358–60.

"Sketches for the Roosevelt Portrait," *The Yale Review,* XXXIX (September 1949), 39–53.

> Translated and published as "Franklin D. Roosevelt: Skizzen für eine Biographie," *Die Amerikanische Rundschau,* VI (December 1949), 75–85.

Review of *Lincoln's Herndon,* by David Donald (New York: Knopf, 1948), *Journal of Southern History,* XV (May 1949), 260–62.

Review of *The Mystery of "A Public Man": A Historical Detective Story,* by Frank Maloy Anderson (Minneapolis: University of Minnesota Press, 1948), *Mississippi Valley Historical Review*, XXXVI (September 1949), 324–25.

1950

Co-edited with Thomas G. Manning, *Government and the American Economy: 1870 to the Present: Select Problems in Historical Interpretation* (New York: Henry Holt, 1950).

> Holt, Rinehart, and Winston published a revised edition in separate booklets in 1960–61: Part 2, "The Railroads," by David M. Potter, revised by E. David Cronon and Howard R. Lamar; Part 5, "Party Politics and Public Action, 1877–1917," by David M. Potter, revised by Howard R. Lamar; Part 7, "The New Deal and Employment," by David M. Potter and William Goetzmann.

> Reviewed by Robert W. Iversen, *Mississippi Valley Historical Review*, XXXVII (September 1950), 358–60.

"An Appraisal of Fifteen Years of the *Journal of Southern History*," *Journal of Southern History*, XVI (February 1950), 25–32.

Review of *The Papers of Thomas Jefferson*, Vol. I: *1760–1776*, edited by Julian P. Boyd; Lyman Butterfield and Mina R. Bryan, associate editors (Princeton, N.J.: Princeton University Press, 1950), *Mississippi Valley Historical Review*, XXXVII (September 1950), 312–14.

Review of *Rustics in Rebellion: A Yankee Reporter on the Road to Richmond, 1861–1865*, by George Alfred Townsend (Chapel Hill: University of North Carolina Press, 1950), *Journal of Southern History*, XVI (November 1950), 548–50.

1951

"Democracy and Abundance," *The Yale Review*, XL (March 1951), 421–39.

> This article, "very much altered," became Chapter V of *People of Plenty* (1954); see p. x of that work.

"John William DeForest," *Papers of the New Haven Colony Historical Society*, X (1951), 188–203.

1952

Review of *The Life of Billy Yank: The Common Soldier of the Union*, by Bell Irwin Wiley (Indianapolis: Bobbs-Merrill, 1952), *The Saturday Review*, April 19, 1952, pp. 27, 50.

Review of *The Federalists: A Study in Administrative History*, by Leonard D. White (New York: Macmillan, 1948); and *The Jeffersonians: A Study in Administrative History*, by Leonard D. White (New York: Macmillan, 1951), *William and Mary Quarterly*, IX (April 1952), 267–71.

Review of *The Citizen Decides: A Guide to Responsible Thinking in Time of Crisis*, by Ralph Barton Perry (Bloomington: University of Indiana Press, 1951); and *Your Rugged Constitution: How America's House of Freedom Is Planned and Built*, by Bruce A. Findlay and Esther B. Findlay (Stanford, Calif.: Stanford University Press, 1950), *The Yale Review*, XLI (June 1952), 636–38.

Review of *Impressions of Lincoln and the Civil War: A Foreigner's Account*, by the Marquis Adolphe de Chambrun; translated by General Adelbert de Chambrun (New York: Random House, 1952), *The Saturday Review*, November 8, 1952, p. 19.

Review of *Lincoln and His Generals*, by T. Harry Williams (New York: Knopf, 1952), *Journal of Southern History*, XVIII (November 1952), 508–9.

1953

"Advertising: The Institution of Abundance," *The Yale Review*, XLIII (September 1953), 49–70.

> This article appeared almost as it stands as Chapter VIII of *People of Plenty* (1954); see p. x of that work. Reprinted in *Advertising Age*, October 4, 1954, pp. 76–82; Poyntz Tyler, ed., *Advertising in America* (New York: H. W. Wilson, 1955), pp. 140–60; and C. H. Sandage and Vernon Fryburger, eds., *The Role of Advertising: A Book of Readings* (Homewood, Ill.: R. D. Irwin, 1960), pp. 18–35.

Review of *Lincoln the President*, Vol. III: *Midstream*, by James G. Randall (New York: Dodd, Mead, 1952); *Abraham Lincoln: A Biography*, by Benjamin P. Thomas (New York: Knopf, 1952); *Lincoln and His Generals*, by T. Harry Williams (New York: Knopf, 1952); *Lincoln Finds a General: A Military Study of the Civil War*, Vol. III: *Grant's First Year in the West*, by Kenneth P. Williams (New York: Macmillan, 1952); *Impressions of Lincoln and the Civil War: A Foreigner's Account*, by the Marquis Adolphe de Chambrun; translated by General Adelbert de Chambrun (New York: Random House, 1952);

Lincoln: A Picture Story of His Life, by Stefan Lorant (New York: Harper Bros., 1952); and *Divided We Fought: A Pictorial History of the Civil War, 1861–1865,* edited by David Donald; Hirst D. Milhollen and Milton Kaplan, picture editors (New York: Macmillan, 1952), *The Yale Review,* XLII (March 1953), 428–35.

Review of *The Great Frontier,* by Walter P. Webb (Boston: Houghton Mifflin, 1952), *American Political Science Review,* XLVII (September 1953), 871–74.

Review of *Stanton: Lincoln's Secretary of War,* by Fletcher Pratt (New York: W. W. Norton, 1953), *The Saturday Review,* October 10, 1953, p. 13.

1954

People of Plenty: Economic Abundance and the American Character (Chicago: University of Chicago Press, 1954). The Charles R. Walgreen Foundation Lectures, University of Chicago, Fall 1950.

Translated by Tokuo Watanabe as *Amerika no Tomi to Kokuminsei* (Tokyo: Kokusai Bunka Kenkyujo, 1957); and by Colette Mesnage as *Les Fils de l'Abondance ou le Caractère National Américain* (Paris: Seghers, 1966). A Spanish version by Sonia Tancredi was issued in 1965 as *La Prosperidad de un Pueblo: Estudio de la Abundancia Económica en Relación con el Carácter Norteamericano* (Mexico: Libreros Mexicanos Unidos, 1965); and a Korean translation was published by Current English Publishing Company, Seoul, in 1969.

Republished as a Phoenix paperback by the University of Chicago Press, 1958. Chapter V, "Democracy and Abundance," reprinted in *Challenge: The Magazine of Economic Affairs,* III (November 1954), 37–41. Chapter IX, "Abundance and the Formation of Character," reprinted in Michael McGiffert, ed., *The Character of Americans: A Book of Readings* (Homewood, Ill.: Dorsey Press, 1964), pp. 146–55; and in Gerald D. Nash, ed., *Issues in American Economic History: Selected Readings* (Boston: D. C. Heath, 1964), pp. 496–500. Parts of Chapter V, "Democracy and Abundance," reprinted in Edward Handler, ed., *The American Political Experience: What Is the Key?* (Lexington, Mass.: D. C. Heath, 1968), pp. 76–82. Parts of Chapters VIII, "The Institution of Abundance: Advertising," and IX, "Abundance and the Formation of Character," reprinted in David R. B. Ross, Alden T. Vaughan, and John B. Duff, eds., *Recent America: 1933 to the Present* (New York: Thomas Y. Crowell, 1971), pp. 230–72. Chapter VII, "Abundance and the Frontier Hypothesis," reprinted in Don E. Fehrenbacher, ed., *History and American Society: Essays of David M. Potter* (New York: Oxford University Press, 1973), pp. 110–34.

Reviewed by Keith Hutchison, *The Nation*, November 6, 1954, p. 411; Gerald Carson, *New York Times Book Review*, November 14, 1954, p. 41; Karl W. Deutsch, *The Yale Review*, XLIV (December 1954), 292–95; George Caspar Homans, *New England Quarterly*, XXVII (December 1954), 553–54; Boyd C. Shafer, *American Historical Review*, LX (January 1955), 380–81; Charles Wegener, *Ethics*, LXV (January 1955), 154–55; Fred A. Shannon, *Mississippi Valley Historical Review*, XLI (March 1955), 733–34; Alice Felt Tyler, *Annals of the American Academy of Political and Social Science*, CCXCVIII (March 1955), 194–95; Dennis H. Wrong, *Canadian Forum*, XXXV (April 1955), 21–22; H. C. Nixon, *American Political Science Review*, XLIX (June 1955), 547–49; C. Wright Mills, *The Saturday Review*, July 16, 1955, p. 19; and Archie H. Jones, *American Journal of Sociology*, LXI (November 1955), 283.

"Nathan Hale and the Ideal of American Union," *The Connecticut Antiquarian*, VI (June 1954), 20–26.

Review of *The Growth of Southern Nationalism, 1848–1861*, Vol. VI of *The History of the South*, by Avery O. Craven (Baton Rouge: Louisiana State University Press, 1953), *American Historical Review*, LIX (January 1954), 392–94.

Review of *Americans Interpret Their Civil War*, by Thomas J. Pressley (Princeton, N.J.: Princeton University Press, 1954), *Journal of Southern History*, XX (August 1954), 400–406.

Review of *A History of the Southern Confederacy*, by Clement Eaton (New York: Macmillan, 1954), *Annals of the American Academy of Political and Social Science*, CCXCVI (November 1954), 176.

1955

"Leisure: The Economic Aftermath," *Challenge: The Magazine of Economic Affairs*, IV (December 1955), 42–46.

Review of *The Social Sciences in Historical Study: A Report*

(New York: Social Science Research Council, 1954), *American Quarterly*, VII (Spring 1955), 78–81.

Review of *The Battle Cry of Freedom: The New England Emigrant Aid Company in the Kansas Crusade*, by Samuel A. Johnson (Lawrence: University of Kansas Press, 1954), *The Historical Bulletin*, XXXVIII (May 1955), 248–49.

Review of *The Liberal Tradition in America: An Interpretation of American Thought Since the Revolution*, by Louis Hartz (New York: Harcourt, Brace, 1955); and *Conservatism in America*, by Clinton Rossiter (New York: Knopf, 1955), *The Yale Review*, XLIV (June 1955), 620–22.

Review of *Lincoln and the Party Divided*, by William Frank Zornow (Norman: University of Oklahoma Press, 1954), *Mississippi Valley Historical Review*, XLII (June 1955), 134–35.

1956

Review of *The American Experience: An Interpretation of the History and Civilization of the American People*, by Henry Bamford Parkes (New York: Knopf, 1955), *American Historical Review*, LXI (January 1956), 472–73.

Review of *The Man Who Elected Lincoln*, by Jay Monaghan (Indianapolis: Bobbs-Merrill, 1956), *The Saturday Review*, April 28, 1956, p. 17.

Review of *Lincoln Reconsidered: Essays on the Civil War Era*, by David Donald (New York: Knopf, 1956), *The Saturday Review*, June 30, 1956, pp. 15–16.

Review of *So Fell the Angels*, by Thomas Graham Belden and Marva Robins Belden (Boston: Little, Brown, 1956), *The Saturday Review*, July 28, 1956, p. 13.

Review of *Henry Watterson: Reconstructed Rebel*, by Joseph Frazier Wall (New York: Oxford University Press, 1956), *American Historical Review*, LXI (July 1956), 984.

Review of *Franklin D. Roosevelt: The Triumph*, by Frank Freidel (Boston: Little, Brown, 1956), *New York Times Book Review*, September 9, 1956, pp. 3, 28.

Review of *Lincoln Finds a General: A Military Study of the Civil War*, Vol. IV: *Iuka to Vicksburg*, by Kenneth P. Williams (New York: Macmillan, 1956), *The Saturday Review*, October 27, 1956, pp. 15, 24.

Review of *Lincoln the President*, Vol. IV: *The Last Full Measure*, by James G. Randall and Richard N. Current (New York: Dodd, Mead, 1955), *Journal of Southern History*, XXII (November 1956), 531–33.

Review of *The Peculiar Institution: Slavery in the Ante-Bellum South*, by Kenneth M. Stampp (New York: Knopf, 1956); *The Negro in American Culture, Based on Materials Left by Alain Locke*, by Margaret Just Butcher (New York: Knopf, 1956); *The Militant South, 1800–1861*, by John Hope Franklin (Cambridge, Mass.: Belknap Press, 1956); and *Segregation: The Inner Conflict in the South*, by Robert Penn Warren (New York: Random House, 1956), *The Yale Review*, XLVI (December 1956), 260–67.

1957
The American Round Table: Discussions on People's Capitalism. Part I. Yale University, November 16–17, 1956. Digest report by David M. Potter, Rapporteur (New York: The Advertising Council, 1957).

The American Round Table: Discussions on People's Capitalism. Part II. "An Inquiry into Cultural Trends Under the American System of Widely Shared Benefits." Yale Club, New York, May 22, 1957. Digest report by David M. Potter, Rapporteur (New York: The Advertising Council, 1957).

> Parts I and II of the symposium were published in a one-volume Japanese translation in 1958.

1958
"Theory Versus Practice in American Values and Performance," in Elting E. Morison, ed., *The American Style: Essays in Value and Performance* (New York: Harper Bros., 1958), pp. 327–33.

"Is America a Civilization?," *Shenandoah: Washington and Lee University Review*, X (Autumn 1958), 18–22.

> Reprinted in Don E. Fehrenbacher, ed., *History and American Society: Essays of David M. Potter* (New York: Oxford University Press, 1973), pp. 222–27.

Review of *The Affluent Society*, by John Kenneth Galbraith (Boston: Houghton Mifflin, 1958), *The Saturday Review*, June 7, 1958, pp. 31–32.

77

Review of *We the People: The Economic Origins of the Constitution,* by Forrest McDonald (Chicago: University of Chicago Press, 1958), *The Saturday Review,* October 11, 1958, pp. 41–42.

1959

"Lincoln and the Meaning of the American Union," in *Abraham Lincoln: Interpretations on the One Hundred and Fiftieth Anniversary of His Birth* (London: United States Information Service, 1959), pp. 37–40.

Review of *Out of Our Past: The Forces That Shaped Modern America,* by Carl N. Degler (New York: Harper Bros., 1959), *The Saturday Review,* February 7, 1959, p. 18.

Review of *The Lincoln Nobody Knows,* by Richard N. Current (New York: McGraw-Hill, 1958), *Mississippi Valley Historical Review,* XLV (March 1959), 671–73.

Review of *The Economic Mind in American Civilization,* Vols. IV–V: *1918–33,* by Joseph Dorfman (New York: Viking, 1959), *The Saturday Review,* July 11, 1959, pp. 14–15.

Review of *The Roosevelt Revolution,* by Mario Einaudi (New York: Harcourt, Brace, 1959), *New York Times Book Review,* August 2, 1959, p. 7.

Review of *Power Without Property: A New Development in American Political Economy,* by Adolf A. Berle, Jr. (New York: Harcourt, Brace, 1959), *The Saturday Review,* September 19, 1959, p. 20.

1960

"The American Economic System," in Lyman Bryson, ed., *An Outline of Man's Knowledge of the Modern World* (New York: McGraw-Hill, 1960), pp. 443–64.

Reprinted as a United States Information Service pamphlet, *The American Economy* (Washington, D.C., 1962), which was translated by Beatriz Moreira Pinto as *Aeconomia Americana* (Rio de Janeiro: Editôra Fundo de Cultura, 1963).

"Jefferson Davis and the Political Factors in Confederate Defeat," in David Donald, ed., *Why the North Won the Civil War* (Baton Rouge: Louisiana State University Press, 1960), pp. 91–114.

Reprinted in *The South and the Sectional Conflict* (1968), pp. 263–86; and in abridged form in Don E. Fehrenbacher, ed.,

The Leadership of Abraham Lincoln (New York: John Wiley, 1970), pp. 62–68.

"National and Sectional Forces in the United States," Chapter XXIII of *The New Cambridge Modern History*, Vol. X: *The Zenith of European Power, 1830–1870*, edited by J. P. T. Bury (Cambridge, Eng.: Cambridge University Press, 1960), pp. 603–30.

"The Six Most Fateful Weeks in American History," in Ralph G. Newman, ed., *Lincoln for the Ages* (Garden City, N.Y.: Doubleday, 1960), pp. 176–81.

Review of *The Metaphysical Foundations of American History*, by Roland Van Zandt (The Hague: Mouton, 1959), *American Historical Review*, LXV (January 1960), 387–88.

Review of *Grant Moves South*, by Bruce Catton (Boston: Little, Brown, 1960), *The Saturday Review*, February 6, 1960, pp. 15–16.

Review of *The Anatomy of American Popular Culture, 1840–1861*, by Carl Bode (Berkeley: University of California Press, 1959), *Virginia Quarterly Review*, XXXVI (Spring 1960), 303–6.

Review of *The War for the Union*, Vol. I: *The Improvised War, 1861–1862*, by Allan Nevins (New York: Scribner's, 1959), *Mississippi Valley Historical Review*, XLVI (March 1960), 718.

Review of *The End of Ideology*, by Daniel Bell (Glencoe, Ill.: Free Press, 1960), *The New Republic*, May 23, 1960, pp. 17–18.

Review of *The Liberal Hour*, by John Kenneth Galbraith (Boston: Houghton Mifflin, 1960), *The Saturday Review*, August 13, 1960, pp. 18, 36–37.

Review of *Three Against Lincoln: Murat Halstead Reports the Caucuses of 1860*, edited by William B. Hesseltine (Baton Rouge: Louisiana State University Press, 1960), *Journal of Southern History*, XXVI (November 1960), 551–53.

Review of *The Burden of Southern History*, by C. Vann Woodward (Baton Rouge: Louisiana State University Press, 1960), *The Yale Review*, L (December 1960), 290–93.

1961

"The Background of the Civil War," in William H. Cartwright and Richard L. Watson, eds., *Interpreting and Teaching*

American History (Washington, D.C.: National Council for the Social Studies, 1961), pp. 87–119. 31st Yearbook of the Council.

> Reprinted in part in Kenyon C. Cramer, ed., *The Causes of War: The American Revolution, the Civil War, and World War I* (Glenview, Ill.: Scott, Foresman, 1965), pp. 107–16; and in much altered form in *The South and the Sectional Conflict* (1968), pp. 88–147.

"Interpreting the Causes of the Civil War," in T. Walter Wallbank and Alastair M. Taylor, *Civilization Past and Present*, 4th ed. (Glenview, Ill.: Scott, Foresman, 1961), pp. 346–48.

"The Enigma of the South," *The Yale Review*, LI (October 1961), 142–51.

> Reprinted in Charles Crowe, ed., *The Age of Civil War and Reconstruction, 1830–1900: A Book of Interpretive Essays* (Homewood, Ill.: Dorsey Press, 1966), pp. 120–26; and in *The South and the Sectional Conflict* (1968), pp. 3–16.

Review of *The Diary of Gideon Welles, Secretary of the Navy Under Lincoln and Johnson*, 3 vols., edited by Howard K. Beale (New York: Norton, 1960), *American Historical Review*, LXVI (January 1961), 474–76.

Review of *No Compromise: The Story of the Fanatics Who Paved the Way to the Civil War*, by Arnold Whitridge (New York: Farrar, Straus, and Cudahy, 1960); *The Crusade Against Slavery, 1830–1860*, by Louis Filler (New York: Harper Bros., 1960); and *Prologue to Sumter: The Beginnings of the Civil War from the John Brown Raid to the Surrender of Fort Sumter*, woven into a continuous narrative by Philip Van Doren Stern (Bloomington: Indiana University Press, 1961), *New York Herald Tribune Book Review*, April 9, 1961, p. 33.

Review of *The Bold Brahmins: New England's War Against Slavery, 1831–1863*, by Lawrence Lader (New York: Dutton, 1961), *New York Herald Tribune Book Review*, June 4, 1961, p. 32.

Review of *Charles Sumner and the Coming of the Civil War*, by David Donald (New York: Knopf, 1960), *American Historical Review*, LXVI (July 1961), 1062–63.

Review of *Turner and Beard: American Historical Writing Reconsidered*, by Lee Benson (Glencoe, Ill.: Free Press, 1960);

Some Twentieth Century Historians: Essays on Eminent Europeans, edited by Samuel William Halperin (Chicago: University of Chicago Press, 1961); and *The American Historian: A Social-Intellectual History of the Writing of the American Past*, by Harvey Wish (New York: Oxford University Press, 1960), *The Nation*, September 2, 1961, pp. 123–25.

Review of *The Divided Union*, by James G. Randall and David Donald (Boston: Little, Brown, 1961), *New York Herald Tribune Book Review*, September 10, 1961, p. 4.

Review of *The Centennial History of the Civil War*, Vol. I: *The Coming Fury*, by Bruce Catton (Garden City, N.Y.: Doubleday, 1961), *The Saturday Review*, November 18, 1961, pp. 20–21.

Review of *Reconstruction After the Civil War*, by John Hope Franklin (Chicago: University of Chicago Press, 1961), *New York Times Book Review*, November 19, 1961, p. 65.

1962

"The Quest for the National Character," in John Higham, ed., *The Reconstruction of American History* (New York: Harper and Row, 1962), pp. 197–220.

Translated by Kiyoo Hamada as "Kokuminsei no Tankyu," in *Amerikashizo no Saikosei* (Tokyo: Ogawa Shuppan, 1970), pp. 249–76.

Reprinted in Michael McGiffert, ed., *The Character of Americans: A Book of Readings* (Homewood, Ill.: Dorsey Press, 1964), pp. 232–44; and in Don E. Fehrenbacher, ed., *History and American Society: Essays of David M. Potter* (New York: Oxford University Press, 1973), pp. 229–55.

"American Women and the American Character," *Stetson University Bulletin*, LXII (January 1962), 1–22.

Reprinted in John A. Hague, ed., *American Character and Culture: Some Twentieth-Century Perspectives* (Deland, Fla.: Everett Edwards, 1964), pp. 65–84; in Edward N. Saveth, ed., *American History and the Social Sciences* (New York: Free Press, 1964), pp. 427–45 (under the title "National Character"); and in Don E. Fehrenbacher, ed., *History and American Society: Essays of David M. Potter* (New York: Oxford University Press, 1973), pp. 278–303.

Translated and published as "Las Mujeres Norteamericanas y

el Carácter de los Norteamericanos," in John A. Hague, comp., *Estados Unidos: Carácter y Cultura: Algunas Perspectivas del Siglo XX* (Mexico City: Compañia General de Ediciones, S.A., 1968), pp. 88–108.

"The Historian's Use of Nationalism and Vice Versa," *American Historical Review*, LXVII (July 1962), 924–50.

Abridged from an article originally written for Alexander V. Riasanovsky and Barnes Riznik, eds., *Generalizations in Historical Writing* (Philadelphia: University of Pennsylvania Press, 1963), pp. 114–66.

Reprinted in *The South and the Sectional Conflict* (1968), pp. 34–83; and in Don E. Fehrenbacher, ed., *History and American Society: Essays of David M. Potter* (New York: Oxford University Press, 1973), pp. 60–108.

Review of *The Edge of Glory: A Biography of General William S. Rosecrans, U.S.A.*, by William M. Lamers (New York: Harcourt, Brace, 1961), *New York Herald Tribune Book Review*, January 28, 1962, p. 8.

Review of *What Is History?*, by Edward Hallett Carr (New York: Knopf, 1962), *The Nation*, February 3, 1962, pp. 104–5.

Review of *The Emerging South*, by Thomas D. Clark (New York: Oxford University Press, 1961), *Mississippi Valley Historical Review*, XLVIII (March 1962), 745–46.

Review of *Lincoln: A Contemporary Portrait*, edited by Allan Nevins and Irving Stone (Garden City, N.Y.: Doubleday, 1962), *The Saturday Review*, April 21, 1962, p. 36.

Review of *Lincoln and the Negro*, by Benjamin Quarles (New York: Oxford University Press, 1962), *New York Herald Tribune Book Review*, May 27, 1962, p. 15.

Review of *Antislavery: The Crusade for Freedom in America*, by Dwight Lowell Dumond (Ann Arbor: University of Michigan Press, 1961); and *A Bibliography of Antislavery in America*, by Dwight Lowell Dumond (Ann Arbor: University of Michigan Press, 1961), *American Historical Review*, LXVII (July 1962), 1063–65.

Review of *White Servitude in Colonial South Carolina*, by Warren B. Smith (Columbia: University of South Carolina Press, 1961), *Manuscripta*, VI (July 1962), 120.

Review of *Beauregard: Napoleon in Gray*, by T. Harry Williams (New York: Collier Books, 1962; originally published in 1955 by the Louisiana State University Press); and *Stonewall Jackson and the American Civil War*, by George F. R. Henderson, abridged by E. B. Long (Greenwich, Conn.: Fawcett Publications, 1962; originally published in 1919 by Longmans, Green), *New York Herald Tribune Book Review*, September 9, 1962, p. 8.

Review of *Jefferson Davis and His Cabinet*, by Rembert W. Patrick (Baton Rouge: Louisiana State University Press, 1961), *Louisiana History*, III (Fall 1962), 372–75.

Review of *The Achieving Society*, by David C. McClelland (Princeton, N.J.: Van Nostrand, 1961), *Business History Review*, XXXVI (Winter 1962), 470–72.

1963

Four entries in the *Encyclopedia Britannica*: "Abolition Movement," Vol. I, pp. 41–42; "Hinton Rowan Helper," Vol. XI, p. 338; "Huey Pierce Long," Vol. XIV, p. 296; and "The South," Vol. XX, pp. 954–58.

"Explicit Data and Implicit Assumptions in Historical Study," in Louis Gottschalk, ed., *Generalization in the Writing of History: A Report of the Committee on Historical Analysis of the Social Science Research Council* (Chicago: University of Chicago Press, 1963), pp. 178–94.

Reprinted in Don E. Fehrenbacher, ed., *History and American Society: Essays of David M. Potter* (New York: Oxford University Press, 1973), pp. 3–26.

"A House Divided," in Louis B. Wright et al., *The Democratic Experience: A Short American History* (Glenview, Ill.: Scott, Foresman, 1963), pp. 174–232. Pagination differs in other editions.

"American Individualism in the Twentieth Century," *The Texas Quarterly*, VI (Summer 1963), 140–51.

Reprinted in Gordon Mills, ed., *Innocence and Power: Individualism in Twentieth-Century America* (Austin: University of Texas Press, 1965), pp. 92–112; and in Don E. Fehrenbacher, ed., *History and American Society: Essays of David M. Potter* (New York: Oxford University Press, 1973), pp. 257–76.

"The Roots of American Alienation," *Emory University Quarterly*, XIX (Winter 1963), 194–218.

> Reprinted in Don E. Fehrenbacher, ed., *History and American Society: Essays of David M. Potter* (New York: Oxford University Press, 1973), pp. 306–33.

Review of *The Politics of Freedom: An Analysis of the Modern Democratic State*, by C. W. Cassinelli (Seattle: University of Washington Press, 1961), *Annals of the American Academy of Political and Social Science*, CCCXLV (January 1963), 199–200.

Review of *The Unregimented General: A Biography of Nelson A. Miles*, by Virginia Weisel Johnson (Boston: Houghton Mifflin, 1962), *The Saturday Review*, February 9, 1963, p. 38.

Review of *A Nation So Conceived: Reflections on the History of America from Its Earliest Visions to Its Present Power*, by Reinhold Niebuhr and Alan A. Heimert (New York: Scribner's, 1963), *New York Times Book Review*, May 19, 1963, p. 22.

Review of *The Radical Right*, edited by Daniel Bell (Garden City, N.Y.: Doubleday, 1963), *The New Leader*, June 24, 1963, pp. 26–27.

Review of *The California Trail: An Epic with Many Heroes*, by George R. Stewart (New York: McGraw-Hill, 1962), *Pacific Historical Review*, XXXII (August 1963), 292–94.

Review of *Antislavery and Disunion, 1858–1861: Studies in the Rhetoric of Compromise*, edited by J. Jeffery Auer (New York: Harper and Row, 1963), *Journal of American History*, L (September 1963), 319–20.

1964

"On Understanding the South: A Review Article," essay on *The Everlasting South*, by Francis Butler Simkins (Baton Rouge: Louisiana State University Press, 1963); and *The Idea of the South: Pursuit of a Central Theme*, edited by Frank E. Vandiver (Chicago: University of Chicago Press, 1964), *Journal of Southern History*, XXX (November 1964), 451–62.

> Reprinted in *The South and the Sectional Conflict* (1968), pp. 17–33.

Review of *Abundance for What and Other Essays*, by David

Riesman (Garden City, N.Y.: Doubleday, 1963), *Virginia Quarterly Review*, XL (Spring 1964), 332–36.

Review of *One Nation Indivisible: The Union in American Thought, 1776–1861*, by Paul C. Nagel (New York: Oxford University Press, 1964), *Journal of American History*, LI (September 1964), 291–92.

Review of *Bandeirantes and Pioneers*, by Vianna Moog (New York: Braziller, 1964); *The Individual and the Crowd: A Study of Identity in America*, by Hendrick M. Ruitenbeek (New York: Thomas Nelson, 1964); and *The Inevitable Americans*, by John Greenway (New York: Knopf, 1964), *The Yale Review*, LIV (October 1964), 124–28.

1965

"Why the Republicans Rejected Both Compromise and Secession," in George Harmon Knoles, ed., *The Crisis of the Union, 1860–1861* (Baton Rouge: Louisiana State University Press, 1965), pp. 90–106.

Reprinted in *The South and the Sectional Conflict* (1968), pp. 243–62.

Review of *An Historian and the Civil War*, by Avery Craven (Chicago: University of Chicago Press, 1964), *Journal of Southern History*, XXXI (May 1965), 207–10.

1966

Co-edited with Curtis R. Grant, *Eight Issues in American History: Views and Counterviews* (Glenview, Ill.: Scott, Foresman, 1966).

Edited "An Account of Pennsylvania [1698]," by Gabriel Thomas, in Vol. I of Daniel J. Boorstin, ed., *An American Primer* (Chicago: University of Chicago Press, 1966), pp. 31–47.

Review of *The Political Economy of Slavery: Studies in the Economy and Society of the Slave South*, by Eugene D. Genovese (New York: Pantheon, 1965), *The Saturday Review*, January 1, 1966, pp. 33–34.

1967

"Canadian Views of the United States as a Reflex of Canadian Values: A Commentary," in S. F. Wise and Robert Craig Brown, eds., *Canada Views the United States: Nineteenth-*

Century Political Attitudes (Seattle: University of Washington Press, 1967), pp. 121–30.

"Depletion and Renewal in Southern History," in Edgar T. Thompson, ed., *Perspectives on the South: Agenda for Research* (Durham, N.C.: Duke University Press, 1967), pp. 75–89.

> Reprinted in *The South and the Sectional Conflict* (1968), pp. 177–98.

"Television, the Broad View: The Historical Perspective," in Stanley T. Donner, ed., *The Meaning of Commercial Television* (Austin: University of Texas Press, 1967), pp. 51–68.

"The Work of Ulrich B. Phillips: A Comment," *Agricultural History*, XLI (October 1967), 359–63. Commentary on an article in that number by Eugene D. Genovese: "Race and Class in Southern History: An Appraisal of the Work of Ulrich Bonnell Phillips."

1968

The South and the Sectional Conflict (Baton Rouge: Louisiana State University Press, 1968).

> Reviewed by Martin Duberman, *New York Times Book Review*, January 12, 1969, pp. 14, 16 (reprinted in Martin Duberman, *The Uncompleted Past* [New York: Dutton, 1971], pp. 75–79); Emory M. Thomas, *The Saturday Review*, April 5, 1969, pp. 58–59; Bell I. Wiley, *Journal of Southern History*, XXXV (August 1969), 394–95; Eugene D. Genovese, *New York Review of Books*, September 11, 1969, pp. 27–30; Chase C. Mooney, *Journal of American History*, LVI (September 1969), 381–82; and George M. Fredrickson, *American Historical Review*, LXXV (June 1970), 1387–92.

"The Civil War in the History of the Modern World: A Comparative View," in C. Vann Woodward, ed., *The Comparative Approach to American History* (New York: Basic Books, 1968), pp. 135–45.

> Translated by Fusashi Yamaguchi as "Nanboku Senso," in Vol. I of *Amerikashi no Shinkanten: Hikakushiteki Kokoromi* (Tokyo: Nan'un-do, 1976), pp. 161–72.

> Reprinted in *The South and the Sectional Conflict* (1968), pp. 287–99.

Review of *The Discovery of Abundance: Simon N. Patten*

and the Transformation of Social Theory, by Daniel M. Fox
(Ithaca, N.Y.: Cornell University Press, 1967), *Journal of
American History*, LV (June 1968), 160–61.

Review of *The Emergence of the New South, 1913–1945*,
Vol. X of *A History of the South*, by George Brown Tindall
(Baton Rouge: Louisiana State University Press, 1967), *Journal
of Southern History*, XXXIV (August 1968), 420–24.

Review of *The Progressive Historians: Turner, Beard, Par-
rington*, by Richard Hofstadter (New York: Knopf, 1968), *New
York Review of Books*, December 5, 1968, pp. 46–48.

> Reprinted in Don E. Fehrenbacher, ed., *History and American
> Society: Essays of David M. Potter* (New York: Oxford Uni-
> versity Press, 1973), pp. 181–91.

1969

"C. Vann Woodward," in Marcus Cunliffe and Robin W.
Winks, eds., *Pastmasters: Some Essays on American Historians*
(New York: Harper and Row, 1969), pp. 375–407.

> Reprinted in Don E. Fehrenbacher, ed., *History and American
> Society: Essays of David M. Potter* (New York: Oxford Uni-
> versity Press, 1973), pp. 135–79.

Review of *Grant Takes Command*, by Bruce Catton (Boston:
Little, Brown, 1969), *The Saturday Review*, March 1, 1969, pp.
29–30.

Review of *Pacific Circle: Proceedings of the Second Biennial
Conference of the Australian and New Zealand American
Studies Association*, edited by Norman Harper (St. Lucia: University of Queensland Press, 1968), *Journal of American History*, LVI (June 1969), 115–16.

Review of *Reconstructing the Union: Theory and Policy
During the Civil War*, by Herman Belz (Ithaca, N.Y.: Cornell
University Press, 1969), *Journal of Southern History*, XXXV
(November 1969), 582–84.

1971

"Changing Patterns of Social Cohesion and the Crisis of Law
Under a System of Government by Consent," in Eugene V.
Rostow, ed., *Is Law Dead?* (New York: Simon and Schuster,
1971), pp. 260–85.

> Reprinted in a slightly different version in Don E. Fehren-

bacher, ed., *History and American Society: Essays of David M. Potter* (New York: Oxford University Press, 1973), pp. 390–418.

"Roy F. Nichols and the Rehabilitation of American Political History," *Pennsylvania History*, XXXVIII (January 1971), 1–20.

> Reprinted in Don E. Fehrenbacher, ed., *History and American Society: Essays of David M. Potter* (New York: Oxford University Press, 1973), pp. 193–217.

Review of *Historians' Fallacies: Toward a Logic of Historical Thought*, by David Hackett Fischer (New York: Harper and Row, 1970), *Journal of Southern History*, XXXVII (February 1971), 86–90.

1972

The South and the Concurrent Majority, edited by Don E. Fehrenbacher and Carl N. Degler (Baton Rouge: Louisiana State University Press, 1972). The 1968 Walter Lynwood Fleming Lectures in Southern History, Louisiana State University.

> Reviewed in an unsigned article in *Virginia Quarterly Review*, XLIX (Winter 1973), xxxiv–xxxv; and by George B. Tindall in *American Historical Review*, LXXVIII (April 1973), 490–92; David L. Smiley in *Journal of Southern History*, XXXIX (May 1973), 273–74; C. Vann Woodward in *Journal of American History*, LX (June 1973), 123–24; Perry H. Howard in *Journal of Negro History*, LVIII (July 1973), 361–63; and Harold M. Hyman in *Political Science Quarterly*, LXXXVIII (December 1973), 757–59.

1973

Division and the Stresses of Reunion, 1845–1876 (Glenview, Ill.: Scott, Foresman, 1973). Vol. IV of the Scott, Foresman American History series.

History and American Society: Essays of David M. Potter, edited by Don E. Fehrenbacher (New York: Oxford University Press, 1973).

> Republished as a paperback by Oxford University Press, 1975. Reviewed by John A. Garraty, *New York Times Book Review*, April 1, 1973, p. 5; *The Yale Review*, LXII (June 1973), x, xii; Cushing Strout, *Journal of Southern History*, XXXIX (August 1973), 425–26; *Virginia Quarterly Review*, XLIX (Autumn

1973), clxiv; Ray Allen Billington, *Journal of American History*, LX (December 1973), 762–63; and George B. Tindall, *American Historical Review*, LXXVIII (December 1973), 1519–21.

1976

The Impending Crisis, 1848–1861, completed and edited by Don E. Fehrenbacher (New York: Harper and Row, 1976). The New American Nation series.

> Reviewed by Eric Foner, *New York Times Book Review*, February 22, 1976, pp. 6–7; and Edward Pessen, *History*, IV (May–June 1976), 138.

Essays on David M. Potter

Sir Denis Brogan, "David M. Potter," in Marcus Cunliffe and Robin W. Winks, eds., *Pastmasters: Some Essays on American Historians* (New York: Harper and Row, 1969), pp. 316–44.

Obituary, *New York Times*, February 19, 1971, p. 41:4.

Obituary, *London Times*, February 26, 1971, p. 16:g.

Obituary, *Journal of Southern History*, XXXVII (May 1971), 341–42.

Don E. Fehrenbacher, Howard R. Lamar, and Otis A. Pease, "David M. Potter: A Memorial Resolution," *Journal of American History*, LVIII (September 1971), 307–10.

Obituary, *Journal of American History*, LVIII (September 1971), 533–35.

Carl N. Degler, "David M. Potter," *American Historical Review*, LXXVI (October 1971), 1273–75.

Don E. Fehrenbacher, "David Morris Potter," in John A. Garraty, ed., *Encyclopedia of American Biography* (New York: Harper and Row, 1974), pp. 873–74.